A Fistful of Agates

Jane Larson Wipf

VANTAGE PRESS
New York

Excerpts from *The Kid's Book of Questions*, Copyright 1988 by Gregory Stock, Workman Publishing Co., Inc., New York, are reprinted with permission. The author also thanks Jim Strommen, Doris and Roland Larson, John Ratzloff, John Graber, and Kirsten Soderlind for permission to reprint and/or utilize their work in the production of this book.

Cover design by Kirsten Soderlind

FIRST EDITION

All rights reserved, including the right of
reproduction in whole or in part in any form.

Copyright © 2004 by Jane Larson Wipf

Published by Vantage Press, Inc.
419 Park Ave. South, New York, NY 10016

Manufactured in the United States of America
ISBN: 0-533-14607-0

Library of Congress Catalog Card No.: 2003092834

0 9 8 7 6 5 4 3 2

In thanks for the deepest love, God's love!
For Mike, Kristin, and Maren with all my love.

With such love you said,
"I love you, Mom."
That was the last time
I heard those words.
Though I longed to hear
them over and over again,
I had to trust in an
unspoken love from then on.

Contents

In Gratitude...	xiii
A Fistful of Agates	1
Open to the Pall of Death	5
The One-Liner	6
The Voice	7
Santa's Hospital Rounds	9
Treasures	10
Zero Recall	11
Waiting	12
Hard-Core Pain	13
The Four-Bedroom Ward	14
Holy Abstinence	15
Doctor Daddy	16
Tender Touches	17
Pain Medication	18
The Lifeline	19
Fear's Anger	21
Packing for Heaven	22
The Welcomed Intrusion	23
Nurses: Love Beyond Boundaries	24
Silent Soldiers	25
Home on Pass	27
Chronic Illness	28
The Viewpoint	29
Out of Control	31
Priorities	32
Torn	33
Impending Separation	34
The Gifts	35
Thank You	36
Tidbits	37
Loving Footprints	38

To Be a Carrier	39
The "Steel Magnolias"	40
Milestones	41
Be Gentle on Yourself	43
Intervention	44
A Choice	46
Cabin Fever	47
The Constant Observer	49
A Day of Reckoning	50
Too Close to the Edge	51
Thank God for Kleenex	53
After Midnight	55
Privacy	56
Round-the-Clock Reassurances	57
Crossword Puzzles, Fishing, and Peanut M&M's	59
Leg Rubs	62
Love Notes	63
Lost and Found	64
The Rubber Banana	66
A Pause in the Hall	67
Counting to Infinity	68
The Healing Issue	69
The Huddle	71
The Little Things	73
A Fear	74
Stark Realities	75
The Lost Lizard	77
Laughter	78
Shootin' the Breeze	79
The Basketball	80
Shots	81
Compassionate Community	83
Broken—Dr. Reaney	85
Letting Go	87
Heart Surgery	88
Keeping Vigil	90
In the Company of Angels	92

No Greater Love	94
Hit On	95
"What Can I Do?"	96
The Dare	97
Anchoring in God's Reality	98
Negotiating with Time	99
Grandma's Stay	101
Ongoing Chatter	102
Oasis of God's Stillness	103
Giving Your Best Shot	104
The Chasm	105
Two Little Tablets	106
Invisible Faith	107
Gaining Entry	109
The Regret	110
Spiritual Getaway	111
Coping Tools	112
His Ways	113
Doctor's Wife	114
The Smile	115
God's Extended Arm	116
A Greater Power	117
The Question	118
Impending Absence	120
The Host	121
All-Alert	122
The Bleed	123
Not Forgotten	124
The Miraculous Nightmare	126
The Guarded High	128
Grandma's Journal	130
An Invitation to Love	131
Nonverbal Dialogue	133
Stay Close	135
The Sweetest Joy	136
Another World	137
Blind	138
Ponderings	139

The Advocates	140
The Brief Visit	141
Renewed in His Love	142
A Spiritual Guide	143
Care Conference	144
One Little Box of Prayers	145
Candle in the Dark	146
A Doctor's Heart	148
"I Have Overcome the World"	149
Courtesy Communication	150
Chocolate Chip Man	151
Room #13	152
Suicidal Roommate	153
Messy	154
Rage	155
The Panel of Glass	156
Go Home	157
In My Arms	158
The Bright Yellow Envelope	159
Terminal	161
The Odds	162
Sick Leave	163
The Red Rose	164
Seeing with the Heart	165
Maren's Birthday	167
Another Day	168
Safe Time	170
An Eye-Opener	172
Sarah's Visit	173
Rock Bottom	174
My Bed	176
Being a Sick Guest	177
Wake-Up Call	178
Well-Wishes	179
Round-the-Clock Vigil	180
The Second Wind	181
There's No Place Like Home	184
Above the Clouds	185

Goddie	186
Mommy's Psalm	187
Doctor's Embrace	189
A Broken Promise	192
Silence	193
Two Visits	194
Love and Sorrow Meet	195
Precious Time	197
Unspoken Love	198
Amnesty	200
Bottles of Hope and Hospice	202
Children	203
The Little things	204
Easter	205
Come On and Fight!	206
Taking a Stand	207
Switching Gears	209
The Consent	210
In Charge	211
The Good-bye	212
Under One Roof	213
Glory	214
Overcome by Sadness	216
Suffering	217
The Empty Chair	218
The Round-up	219
Holiday Plus	220
Please	221
Long-distance Dream	222
Surrender	223
God's Mystery	224
In the Backyard	225
Christ Present	226
Walking in the Rain	227
It Is Finished	228
Good-Night	230
Grief	233

In Gratitude . . .

To my faithful parents, Roland and Doris Larson, for their supportive wisdom and ongoing tender love. And for Mom's endless typing of the original manuscript which brought many shared tears. Furthermore, dipping into my mom's journal aided in my storytelling!

To my dear god-child, Michelle Stimpson, who lovingly compiled the final writing on computer.

God knows each and every one of you who has crossed our paths and who has encouraged, helped, and loved us. I am so deeply grateful!

And to Mike, Kristin, Maren, and Tommy . . . my anchors of home and heaven. Words barely nick how appreciative I am, and how much I love you!

A Fistful of Agates

"Mommy, come and wipe me!"

As the phrase pierced the night, deep sleep had already begun to settle in. The bed was so cozy. It had warmed quickly as our bodies lay together.

Mike awoke. Grunting at his forgetfulness, he rolled away from me, reaching for the alarm clock, punching in numbers for a 5:30 A.M. wake-up.

As his arm enfolded me once again, a wee voice repeated her request.

"Coming, Kristin," I responded.

Donning a robe, I reluctantly made a labored move to the bathroom across the hall where our three-year-old delight sat patiently.

Task completed, I rocked Kristin in her room as night became familiar to her once again. Glancing at two-year-old Maren sound asleep on the egg-crate mattress on the floor, I laid Kristin down next to her sister. Our chicks were gathered and safe under one roof. It was a peaceful feeling.

Mike was snoring by the time I slipped back into bed. Exhaustion was a part of life for both of us. Summertime wasn't too far away, and Mike would begin his sixth and final year of a urology residency. After much hard work, school, and sacrifice, a new light at the end of a long tunnel was about to appear. Smiling, I pulled the bed sheet up under my chin.

A hard kick in my belly scattered my thoughts. Great with child, I was glad our younger daughter and I had recently ended breast-feeding so as to make way for the demands of number three, soon to arrive in June.

All was still in the tiny dark apartment except for a cool breeze from the window above our heads. As the curtains danced with a purposeful grace, I finally fell asleep. My hands had found their place alongside my husband's hands, encircling the womb that had thus far carried three of our children.

Late that night, the dream I'd had several times before would come to me one more time:

> God's compassionate, yet sovereign voice told me, *"There will be a health problem with this baby, but be at peace. My hand is on him."*

*   *   *

"This baby's coming fast."
Broad shoulders on this kid required an extra hefty push.
"It's a boy!"

Umbilical cord still attached, Thomas Michael was placed atop Mom. It was a glorious landing—torso to torso—hearts beating close. The protective wraps were many and awesome... from uterus to placenta, layered with blood, vernix and amniotic fluid. This flesh of our flesh was both a dream and a reality.

Birth is so harsh, yet so intimate. Mike and I basked in this miraculous event. We, too, felt close. The moment was so sure, so solid, so filled with promise.

As a parent, it's natural to make plans and figure that you'll be able to control a good chunk of life. But, I knew life was simply a twinkling of an eye in the scheme of things.

Only God knew ahead.

Would Tommy play football or choose to wear tattoos? Would he be moody? Would he love art? Would he be kind? Would he be a hermit? Would he be gay? Would he love the garden? Would his little fists someday clench prison bars?

No matter what, even if we, as parents, promised to love him and somehow couldn't, I knew God would love him. God would never fail him.

Within hours after delivery, I would be abruptly reminded of God's message to me in the dream that I had while pregnant.

Staph bacteria ran rampant throughout Tommy's 8+-pound frame and his eyes were swollen shut. He and I were immediately isolated alone in a room. Though excited about this little one, I felt a 180-degree shift.

Little did we know, a genetic defect in my X-chromosome had marked my son. It would harness our child with a disease in which the white cells don't kill certain bacteria and fungi. Staph was just the beginning. As Mike and I held our precious newborn, at the same time—we were cradling the enemy.

There will be a health problem with this baby, but be at peace. My hand is on him.

I continued to be reminded of God's divine presence. A verse repeatedly appeared on a hospital food tray that said, *"My grace is sufficient for you, for my power is made perfect in weakness"* (2 Cor. 12:9).

For over seven and a half years, Tommy fought a losing battle against the onslaught of multiple infections. A day came on April 24, 1990, when I held him for the last time. Our hearts beat close like on the day he was born.

Exactly when Tommy's heart stopped, I'm not sure. But, a while before his breath ceased, I could feel Tommy leave his body.

News of Tommy's death traveled quickly, and the front door to our home became a holy place. Responsive love from many poured in the next couple of days. One of those was a little six-year-old comrade of Tommy's. Up the stair steps and through our front door he came. Sheepishly, but determined to bestow his condolences, Paul pulled his arm from behind his back and triumphantly extended his fist out to me.

As his hand slowly opened, there in his sweaty palm was a fistful of tiny agates...some sticking to his fingers. As I got down on my knees, Paul transferred the warm, wet agates to my hand. They were like a scatter of detached rosary beads, reminding me of prayers offered up that have incredible power. Paul and his gift were love...in human form. So pure, so simple, so good.

No vigilance or earthly effort on our part could save Tommy.

God has never promised justice here on earth. Our journey with Tommy has taught us to surrender and to wait on God's power. In our acknowledging His sovereignty, God helps us touch the silver lining.

Open to the Pall of Death

Grief and loss are a part of all of our lives. Their shadows permeate into our thoughts even though we spend most of our time trying to elude them. Through work, entertainment, music, and personal relationships, we seek escape. But eventually, grief and loss return to our thoughts and being; they must be confronted.

This book and these letters are the thoughts and expressions of one mother—my wife—who has opened herself to contemplating the pall of death. In doing so, she has found a meaning and depth to life not often found. The story brims with the simple and yet profound reflections on a mother's experience of her child's illness and death. Indeed, the letters are like a child's agates—ordinary... but priceless. Though the details of her story are unique, the experience is not. My hope and prayer are that this story will help you embrace your grief and losses so that you, too, might be free.

—Michael Wipf

The One-Liner

As I begin unfolding Tommy's last four months and the aftermath of death, I must set the stage by telling you that this child was encapsulated by a love of God and a sense of humor—two effective weapons I would find all over again in my life and reclaim.

Here's Grandpa Roland's favorite story of Tommy:

When Tommy was three years old, his grandpa picked him up in his 1971 VW camperbus for a trip to a nearby shopping center. As they drove down the street with the radio blaring, a good deal of advertising was being aired: "See the new Volvo today; drive the new Volvo . . . " and on and on. Tommy turned to Grandpa and said, "You don't got one of those, do you, Gramps?"

Grandpa said, "No, this is a VW—it's called a Volkswagen." After a long pause, Tommy thoughtfully and matter-of-factly said, "Grandpa, you don't have a vulva. You and I are boys. We have penises. My mommy's got a vulva."

Delightfully cracked up, Grandpa Roland could scarcely wait to share this one-liner with me.

The Voice

Dear Tommy,

It was Monday, December 18, 1989, at 3:15 P.M. that we were scheduled to see Dr. Stephen Marker for a follow-up visit regarding the anemia that had been discovered two months before.

The clinic was running late. I grew anxious as my mind reflected on the fever that you had the night before, tipping me off to an inkling that something else was going on in your body.

When our turn finally came, Dr. Marker looked tired from a long day and a cold. To top it off, here we were with a chest x-ray that showed some mass around your lung, signaling hospital admittance.

As if it were your first day of camp, you eagerly packed your duffel bag that next morning. I'm not sure of all that was going through your mind this time, but you assumed it would be a short stay and looked forward to some video games that you had played there before.

I remember holding you before we left. Kristin and Maren were already off to school, so we spent some alone time in the rocking chair. Christmas was near, and we had already put up the tree together as a family. Now you were about to leave and you smiled, waving to the full green fir, "Bye, Tree." Somehow that gesture tore at my heart.

Bursting with boyish energy, you had that All-American flair with your white tennies and sweats and strong body.

Pulling out of the driveway that morning, I felt a stillness, and then like some sort of awesome presence—a voice with a message, *"He's not coming home this time."* It moved me enough to stop halfway down the street and pause in a neighbor's driveway. If it were true, I wanted to take a photo of you. When I asked you, Tommy, you were anxious to move on, so we did. That voice was to haunt me from then on, and yet it prepared me that perhaps you *were* leaving . . . not to return.

With vacation coming and what I figured would be a possible two- to three-week stay, I wanted you and your friends to be able to say good-bye. So, we made a stop at school where your fellow first-graders could talk with you and hug you and see that you looked good and would be back soon.

Santa's Hospital Rounds

Dear Tommy,

For the next three weeks, the whirl and fatigue of Christmastime laid its mark. Daddy was working and Grandpa Roland and Grandma Doris were about to embark on a long-awaited vacation.

The day you arrived at the hospital, Santa Claus was making rounds as well as the doctors. Remember how reluctant you were to get a photo with him? I asked you to be nice to Santa because he was just trying to cheer people up. That photo I would treasure all too soon and wished it were you and me, instead of you and Santa.

You were put on the routine antibiotic treatment for the fungus, aspergillus. We assumed within a matter of weeks, that you'd be home.

Treasures

Dear Tommy,

Christmas Eve must seem a bit foggy to you. We took you home on a pass to Grandpa and Grandma's where everyone gathered to celebrate.

Wrapped in blankets, you were carried by us into familiar territory. Candlelight and the smells of evergreen and Christmas dinner blended into a homey embrace.

You were placed right into Grandma's arms to rock you as your temperature once again began to soar. Soon, I laid you in bed and there you slept a long time...so contrary to your nature and *especially* on the night that kids were wired for. Dad and I quietly worried. I think all hearts were knitted in that same concern.

After a nap and Tylenol, you perked up considerably. I held you in my lap as you ate a small portion of leftovers. We listened to the Christmas story and then made a dash for the gifts under the tree.

Well, you must have been feeling pretty lousy not to have wanted to stay home overnight on Christmas Eve. So, knowing Santa came around the hospital, you decided to make sure you were bodily counted for, so you could be a recipient of the goods given out. Ha! You also made sure we would bring your stocking and gifts from home which you tore open in one excited swoop. The two gifts I remember the most were a small panda bear from the hospital donations, which you named "Baby"...and the blue Bible we gave you that you had asked for.

I look back now and think, here is this little stuffed animal of yours at my bedside. None of those gifts you took with you to heaven—only the love that came amidst the giving of it all and the promises in that little Bible. *"Thy Word is a lamp unto My feet and a light unto My path."*

Zero Recall

Dear Tommy,

    These first weeks felt like a blur in some ways. I remember staring a lot at the TV or a magazine, having zero recall of what I had just watched or read. My mind grew intensely focused and began to lurk in the unknown—dwelling on the subtle signs of a son whom I knew was not getting better.

Waiting

Dear Tommy,

Time began to tick away, and amidst the CAT scans and x-rays, I felt an urgency to get on with it. The lung mass appeared stabilized—perhaps even smaller, but waiting in a pocket of timelessness was not easy, was it?

In the midst of a lull, a friend from school loaned you a Nintendo game. What pure joy for you, eh? You became a whiz at it and worried that it would tire you to the point of getting sicker. Remember you once told me, "Mom, take this away—I think I'm getting addicted to it!" At another point, though, you reassured me, saying, "It helps take my mind off surgery."

A blessing and a curse it was! It felt like you got *so* focused on Nintendo that you seemed to "wall us out" at times.

It must have been hard to just be you when you had three roommates and their families around and medical people and guests in and out, and you were battling a war inside your body, still trying to be a little host. Even in the pain and nausea of all those months, you tried to juggle it all.

I remember one time you were in the playroom and you lay against a huge stuffed teddy bear—four times bigger than you—and then sandwiched yourself with another bear on top of you. I panicked when we couldn't find you at first. But, it must have felt good to momentarily disconnect and have a haven where you could just be suspended in nothingness and softness.

Maybe that's why home was such a luxury—to go out on pass, trundle off into our bed, submerge in home sheets and quilts, and doze off for hours at a time.

Hard-Core Pain

Dear Tommy,

Before Grandpa and Grandma left for vacation, you got to come home for a night. I think Dr. Marker sensed that we needed a break. So, we all celebrated Kristin's eleventh birthday as your temperature grew higher. You were hunched over, wrapped in a blanket, as she blew out her candles.

You cried so hard the next day when I said we had to go back to the hospital. The hospital time had become long—no longer just another quick trip. The hard-core stuff began to hit.

Pancreatitis came first—a horrific pain that had no goal like childbirth, just pure pain. Initially, the intense pain in your belly was a puzzle. It seemed as though there was a guardedness about how to treat you or what pain medicine to give you without a diagnosis. I became defensive, and I felt at times there was judgment on you by others—that perhaps you were conjuring up some symptom to get more morphine. But, it became obvious that that wasn't true. "Mommy, it feels like someone is stabbing me with a knife. It feels like someone is killing me!"

Time and again, the wrap of protection I had around my children—or thought I had—eluded me. I realized I was often at the mercy of a situation, or at least vulnerable. I had to let God take over.

Due to a complication of a medication, the pancreatitis was treated by removal of the drug, and you were put on IV nutrients to keep you fed. I remember you requesting for me to keep bringing you "Fun Fruits." And, I also remember that when little friends would come to visit you, your top drawer would open, and you would hand them a packet of those Fun Fruits. In your own pain, you still reached out and gave.

The Four-Bedroom Ward

Dear Tommy,

The community that evolved within our four-bed ward amazed me. It was there that you first met Matt. Acquiring a muscle disease at about age nine, he was there in a wheelchair... struggling like you to try to be normal, to rise above the shadow of chronic illness and be a kid. I'm glad his mom and I exchanged addresses that day. In time, our friendship would be a Godsend.

And there was Andy, the boy who came in with a major stroke—who had a one percent chance of survival. I thought for sure *you* would be going home in a matter of weeks. But, it was Andy who awoke and beat the odds. Andy's progress and eventual smile gave me peace and hope as our darkness began to close in. Together with Andy's family, we shared medical updates of our sons, birthday cake, and a visit from Andy's puppy.

And Brandon—who was older and wiser and lassoed with a brain disease—took you under wing as a little brother. Brandon and his crew weathered the hours alongside us, too.

Despite the intermittent chaos of four families in one room with different sleep times, TV requests, visitors, and medical agendas, there was a time and a place to savor the four-bed ward. With Daddy's long work hours and your sisters' schedules, it was a good feeling to leave for a while and know that you wouldn't be entirely alone and without people, conversation, and entertainment. I felt like a den mother at times.

I smile when I think about the closed circuit TV programs. I was helping Andy one day with a game sheet. You sure got jealous and said I was *always* helping Andy. It must have been hard to be amidst such continual change and the unknowns of each day. You were loaded with surprises—that's for sure! I think we both just wanted to run away, don't you?

Holy Abstinence

Dear Tommy,

Nodes appeared on your head and under your chin. They were itchy, weren't they? The looming fear was: *What was this organism anyway?* It appeared to be spreading as surgery became more and more of a reality. The medicine wasn't working, and a needle biopsy was a possible option as a prelude to surgery. Risks were being weighed, and time ticked on. It was January 18, 1990.

How weird it must have been for you to be on morphine and IV food without the pleasures I so took for granted—good health and being able to eat.

One night when I had left the hospital early, you called me to find out what we were eating for dinner. As I began to give you a blow-by-blow account, your inquiries became of the greatest detail. A seven-year-old fantasizing about food! I felt a surge of laughter and at the same time a stark realization that your world was certainly one that I did not understand. Your involuntary abstinence from food made me wonder that perhaps your bodily fasting created a holier realm in you—a clearance from external things. I believe it was a transition point for you as you locked into new survival techniques and strengths that had never been called on before within that precious heart and mind and soul of yours.

We, too, had to switch gears, Tommy...for we began to feel the panic and the reality of being on the edge of death.

Doctor Daddy

Dear Tommy,

Saturday at 2:00 P.M., Pastor Groehler came to anoint you. It was a special moment in time, and of prayer, with family. He gave you a little white handmade baptismal towel that he had used on your head. You handed it to me and asked that it be put on your dresser at home. It was a gesture that helped me link you back home.

These days we're still moving with caution. Daddy was weary from the stress of work, coupled with the worry over your lack of medical progress. It was always a joy to see him, wasn't it? There were benefits to Daddy being a doctor. We had good insurance to pay for the ongoing bills, and on the days he worked at Children's Hospital, he could come up to visit after operating. I remember Daddy in his scrubs bringing me a bite to eat or you a hug . . . and we'd just *be* . . . together.

One time, when Doctor Dad told of his long day at work, Kristin's little quip said it all: "Where's the part where you come home?"

No patient waits longer for the doctor than the physician's own loved ones waiting at home.

Tender Touches

Dear Tommy,

　Days of needle pokes, pain, nausea, and fever spikes began to wear on us all. Both Dad and I often told you we wished that we could have the pain for you. You would quickly respond, "I wish you could, too."

　Your node biopsy—induced in general anesthesia—on your head and chin was soon over. Then, we had to wait for a period of days for a culture. So many unknowns. So many "ifs." But, this solid action of checking out the nodes made me feel like something was being done. I felt like I was on a glider, no longer anxious.

　Remember Dr. Stafford, your stomach doctor? When we first met him, he sat on your bed and drew a little creature on your hand in ink. That was his trademark and one that made you feel safe . . . like a children's handshake-type of greeting.

　Dr. Stafford was the doctor who would run into Dad and me in the evening or in the stairwell and shake his head at what we were amidst, and at the same time verbally encourage us along with such tenderness.

　One day he told me, "What a little heartbreaker. Tommy's quite a guy." Then he remarked on your good attitude, Tommy.

Pain Medication

Dear Tommy,

103° and 104° temps were not uncommon, and despite the possibility of drug fevers, Dr. Belani didn't think so. I sure was glad to have Dr. Marker and Dr. Belani as your core physicians.

We continued to wait.

The pancreatitis pain continued to manifest itself, and once again I felt angered if anyone alluded to your having drug-seeking behavior. I knew that if you said you were in pain, you were! For years, we had talked about medication at home and about only taking it if you really needed it. We became real open about it when you were at home on home-care getting IV Amphotericin and morphine. Once at dinnertime you had said, "I wish I could have more of that sleep medicine. It makes my neck feel funny."

Liz, the nurse from home-care, referred me to an article on pain that helped me in understanding that tolerance or physical dependence is not equivalent to "addiction."

The times you would get canker sores (often it was every ten days—a new batch of 10 to 20 at a time), you were careful even then with Tylenol use. It definitely helped take the edge off, but sometimes you would say you were fine—but, I know you could have used some relief. Keeping busy helped with those yucky canker sores. I often wished I could have done more than give you Tylenol and water, but you would respond with assurance: "That's all you can do, Mom."

Remember the time in the kitchen when we talked about friendships? I said, "If your friends don't love you as you are, then maybe the friendship isn't real." With sunglasses on and your tummy sticking out under your t-shirt, you declared loudly with confidence, "Well, Mom, I'm drug-free and smoke-free, ya know!" Ha!

The Lifeline

Dear Tommy,

A CAT scan revealed a mass on your kidney that looked about the same size as the last scan. More questions to ponder...

Fungus was cultured out from the head nodes—possibly aspergillus. If lung surgery was the next step, then your port-a-cath would have to be removed and replaced with a new one, because the old one could be infected with fungus, too, and carry it into your body.

I remember when your port-a-cath was put in before you started kindergarten. It was a beautiful option versus getting stuck with IV's all the time. You said, "I'm glad they 'thunk' of something fast!"

In your eagerness to share your new chest piece, you shared it for "Show and Tell." I thought it was neat that you could be open about it, and yet I also knew your deep desire to be like everyone else and be treated as such—not with pity or extra attention.

Many times you just didn't want us to talk about your immune problem with others. We tried to respect that and treat you normally, but there was a worry that often cast itself over you. Sometimes I needed to share and talk about it because chronic illness, like death, permeates everything.

Remember back in the spring of '89 when I was trying to heparnize your port-a-cath with a syringe one night? It was my second time and the needle slipped. I felt like such a failure and even dreamed that night of being shot in the chest with a gun.

Anyway, you saw my tears of despair and frustration and gave me a big hug and said, "It's okay, MOM."

Then, the next time I did it, I paid you a dollar. I really wanted to overcome the botched-up job. The dollar seemed a fair trade at that point for your vote of confidence...or at least for your peace of mind that all wouldn't be lost in the deal.

Ever so small (about the size of a nickel), it was under the skin on your chest, I secretly couldn't wait until the day the port-a-cath came out for good. Initially, you guarded that spot when we would hug, but then, it became part of you and we knew it was a lifeline, in a sense, for many meds to pass through . . . lines of hope to make you well.

And in the last hospitalization, I think you best dramatized your feelings as well as ours one night. Remember I had tried to get you into some play therapy by putting a port-a-cath, IV needles, and a tubeline into your three-foot stuffed gorilla that Uncle Tom gave you? Sometime later, when we were out of the room, we learned that you had ripped the whole wad of tubes and tape off Murphy, the gorilla, and flung it across the room.

I felt glad that your anger had found another release—but also felt lost in that expression because I had to admit our little family was under fire and in great turmoil by an invisible organism that seemed to have the reins.

I missed your jetlike moves as you grew sicker—the way you practically flew down the hall, unhindered by the fact that you had to tote an IV pole alongside. I missed your touch and your hugs because so often you couldn't be held or laid down with because you hurt so much.

Fear's Anger

Dear Tommy,
    One night we left each other with cross words and in quite a huff. Morphine and amphotericin made you edgy, plus you must have felt like hell, hurting and vomiting continuously. I think that night I was suddenly so scared of our separation... of your possible death. I had never left angry before. That was one thing that Dad and I tried never to do with one another—go to bed angry or leave home mad.
    And I left you unresolved, raw open-ended. I was tired of chronic illness and no longer had control. I wanted so badly to tell you everything would be okay. I guess we were both on separate journeys of beginning to grieve death.
    I remember at night in bed with Dad, both of us in tears. My cries were like primal screams at one point. It felt like something was tearing away deep within my belly... like one's soul ripping out of the physical. Daddy and I would talk openly of your dying. What a relief to share our hopes and our fears... even of imagining your body underground and decaying. That was the horrible human part that we had to begin grappling with. Our minds had to have free play with *all* angles as we ached so deeply.
    Time and time again, I realized that my whole basis of parenthood is touch!
    One night I dreamed I held you. Then, the next morning I prayed about that desire. That same day at the hospital, you let me hold you! I was in my glory! I related my dream to you as we rocked and you grinned. "You never told me that before!," and, "I didn't even know!" You, too, had dreamed a similar thing that night and eagerly shared that you came home for a few hours and forgot to go back to the hospital! I laughed.
    Healing came in other ways, and this was one of those times... to hold you, my son, in my arms. How simple, how grand! I knew then that God had the reins.

Packing for Heaven

Dear Tommy,

Packing for heaven! That's it. You were always getting ready. I remember calling Children's Hospital late one night to say prayers again and tell you I loved you. I asked if you wanted to hear a Bible verse. You responded yes. Then, we read another and another and another. I felt like I was in the presence of a young squirrel—quietly gathering and storing nuts for a long winter. You had God's Word hidden in your heart. Yes, that's it. You were packing for heaven!

The Welcomed Intrusion

Dear Tommy,

There was a notice one day for Dad and me that the social worker had come. Immediately, my whole defense system triggered all alarms, and I felt hot and cornered inside. *Social worker.* That title signaled to me that we had maybe done something wrong or that some problem has arisen that we were being confronted with. I tossed the mention of him out of my mind as best I could.

Then one day, *he* came while I was with you, Tommy. You were hurting and we had drawn the drape partway in the dusky atmosphere of late afternoon for you to take a nap.

It was in those next twenty minutes that my fears and my apprehension about social workers melted away.

As Jerome spoke, I knew he cared. In the calm exchange of conversation, I realized he was there for *me*. As he understood it, he presented our situation with an urgency and in words that I hadn't heard before. He verbalized and validated the crisis we were in and wanted me to know that he was there if I needed him. I had become so bottled up inside and focused on helping you that I had almost forgotten my own needs to take care myself.

I remember that we had to end our dialogue, but I sensed that he would stay in touch. I hoped so. I didn't want to lose him.

Dad initially seemed bothered about Jerome, but I think that held true for any seemingly "extra" people who latched on to our situation, for in time we became inundated with nurses, doctors, surgeons, and other hospital people. In a way, it would plague us. In another way, it gave us a tight-knit community of people whom we grew to love dearly.

And so, Jerome, being one of those people, represented for me—a male contact as well that I cherished with Daddy working so many hours.

Jerome became one of the most welcomed intrusions.

Nurses: Love Beyond Boundaries

Dear Tommy,

How I would love to have given each one of the nurses a yellow rose! They were often the hour-by-hour moral support and physical presence for us. As time passed, the attachment to everyone grew. The seemingly little gestures made my day . . . a smile, a hug, a kind word, being handed a Kleenex. When all is gone, that's what is left—a love that outlasts struggle and disease—right, Buddy?

Some of the best moments of being uplifted and encouraged were in the stairwell or in the parking ramp. Just a simple, "How are you?" was not a surface question anymore. People really hurt with us. I remember seeing Giselle, one of the nurses nicknamed "Pearls," in the parking ramp. Dad, the girls, and I were getting out of our van and I had just gotten my tears under control when her eyes caught mine. She hugged me, and I sobbed. There was no need for words. She was in the battle with us.

It's like an old anniversary card I found that I wrote to Daddy a few years back: "We're special together. I love you, Mike! It's neat to know amidst the cruddy times and the joyful times, our heart is centered in love . . . in a Creator whom I do question sometimes—but in whose hands I feel nowhere more secure. Jane."

Silent Soldiers

Dear Tommy,

Silent Soldiers. That is the phrase I gave to your sisters, Kristin and Maren. Like you, they have weathered the unpredictability and unknowns of your disease.

I remember the first year of your life while we still lived in California. It was rugged—in and out of the hospital, month after month. The girls would be farmed out to three friends who were a part of the mothers' play group that we had become involved with. Karen, Mary, and DeeDee soon became like sisters to me. Combined with their own wee ones, each woman really sacrificed a large portion of her days to help us.

Sometimes Kristin and Maren would come home late at night—finally reunited with Daddy, whose urology residency demanded almost his all, and a mom who feared for the life of her son. Many times while you camped out at the hospital, the girls would snuggle in bed with us, having been void of my former twenty-four-hour physical presence. Once in a while, Kristin would scream—a release for a three-year-old who couldn't verbalize fully how hard she had tried to be the perfect guest all day at someone else's home—maybe typical for a first child, and yet so demonstrative of the situation. Molded in love and hardship, there comes a great time when the brokenness seeds itself and multiplies.

I witnessed this in one of the most precious times I have ever known.

We came home late one night when you were six, Maren was eight, and Kristin was nine. It was another hospital stay for you, and the girls met us at the top of the stairs, leading us into the kitchen. It was 10:00 P.M., and the girls sat us down at a table decked with plates, tea, and a muffin. Name tags stood in front of each of us marked "Dad" and "Mom." As we turned over the hand-penciled love notes, Daddy's said, "Kiss

Mom." Mine said, "Kiss Dad."

Then, a candle was lit, the room darkened, and with a squeeze on our shoulders, the girls said, "We're going to bed. We think you need some time alone."

Home on Pass

Dear Tommy,

Passes home were a piece of heaven, weren't they? (Would you still use that phrase, "A piece of heaven," now that you are there?)

The end of January was the last time I remember you being in your room at home. We snuggled together in your bed for a time, warm with fever—but cozy, until it was time to go back to the hospital. Curled up in a fetal position, you rolled your eyes teasingly toward me as if to say, "I dare you to make me go."

Finally when you were coaxed to go into the living room, I danced to music with you as I held you in my arms. Detached from the world around us, we whirled in glee and I laughed as we had done countless times before . . . unaware that this would be our last dance.

Chronic Illness

Dear Tommy,

One morning I had big plans for the day. Then, the toilet overflowed.

It reminded me of chronic illness. The toilet overflows a lot. Plans get detoured. How you handle your attitude helps. And, as in a marathon, you pace yourself differently than running the 440.

Like Dr. Marker said, "Normal isn't necessarily better." I must agree—I think one sees life's scenery in a way that trims the fat and sets one's priorities.

Ha! Like cleaning the house. During your last hospitalization, Tommy, twenty-one-year-old cousin Michelle said, "Well, I can tell how things are going by how the house looks!" It's true—my desk and the dining room table were stacked with papers, bills, and laundry, surrounded by dying plants. Who knows what else was piling up?

Chronic illness in a family does leave its wake. As eight-year-old Maren summed it up best as you spent another chunk of time in the hospital and she and her sister were often left at home, "Mom, I feel like my heart is broken!"

Chronic illness. No longer am I fighting for hunger and world peace, but for a boy's life and quality of existence.

To mask oneself with a type of "normalcy" and humor is a challenge. I finally learned to ask for help, to take care of myself, and to network and reach out for what I need—whether it's emotional, physical, or spiritual.

The Viewpoint

Dear Tommy,

An echocardiogram was taken of your heart and valves to see that the mass hadn't penetrated the heart's walls. Remember, you got to keep the photo of your heart and put it up on the walls with your own artwork and artwork of your friends and class at school?

It was a year before you died, and while on vacation we asked you three kids some questions posed in "The Kids' Book of Questions." One stated:

Imagine you got hit by a car and could be saved only by a special operation. The operation would give you a normal, happy life, but would unfortunately cause you fifteen minutes of terrible, stabbing pain every morning when you awoke. Would you want to have the operation?

You all said you would have the operation, but you, Tommy, had second thoughts. "Maybe I want to go and live with Jesus," you said. You knew so well what it was like to have excruciating pain.

The pancreatitis was your stabbing pain and was unheard of in this situation—a real puzzle. It was found to be due to a medicine, which was stopped. Then, they began an aggressive use of amphotericin, which is like chemotherapy. I remember in the beginning your turning blue-lipped and very cold and shaky. The nurse and I would huddle you up into layers of blankets until the fever began to come down. Morphine helped those side effects. The drug's nickname fit true: "Ampho Terrible."

In time, we had yet another prayer service in which you had so many hands on your head that it was obviously very uncomfortable. Afterwards, you went nuts scratching there and wet down your hair! You made us all laugh, Tommy!

Seeing family and friends pop in was a real boost and something to look forward to—to pass the time, take my mind off everything, and be encouraged. Uncle Dan and Aunt Mikki even came with their Pomeranian twice! Like the Humane Society visits, these furry creatures gave a buffer; a distraction and a reminder of home. They also posed no threats of needle pokes, etc.

Out of Control

Dear Tommy,

On March 11, 1990, I dreamed of our family on a huge amusement park wild ride that tilted at an angle and went up high. It was flat and open (vulnerable). As we spun up to the top, you were unstrapped, Tommy, and wandered over toward the edge. Out of my reach, I screamed in panic for Dad to grab you (mad that he missed). Over the edge, you fell far below. (That dream of your falling over edges has been repeated over the years.)

In a horrible panic, my heart fell as I raced to where you now lay... thin, naked, and broken arms and legs in the darkness. I scooped your limp body into my arms and raced to the church. There it was dark and silent. It was so lonely. In desperation, I placed a call for help to Dad's partner, Earle, who had cancer. I couldn't dial.

It's weird how premonitions emerged in dreams, etc.—like God was perhaps preparing me. At the same time, as dark as the next days and months became, we were totally in God's hands. We had lost all control.

Like I would later hear—it was in those pitch-black days that God's wing was over us the closest. The darkness was His shadow of grace, love, and protection. People may poo-poo that phrase that "God protects," but I witnessed even in the nausea, the screams of pain, the penetrating organism—that there was a spiritual reassurance in both you and me, Tommy, that transcends words and life here on earth. I guess that is what Christ talks about—the "peace that passes all understanding."

Priorities

Dear Tommy,

Basically, Dad and I were pretty sedate and not very assertive in the beginning of this last illness. Maybe we were too easygoing. But, one thing that I did stand up for was when tutoring was suggested. You were so conscientious. About that time when you would set aside your homework in exhaustion, I knew you were really sick. You even told me that you hoped you could do some home-schooling the rest of the year.

I voiced my feelings to Jerome, the social worker, and essentially said, "The heck with tutoring. This kid is only in first grade and he can catch up this summer—if he's even alive. This kid could be dying!"

The pressure was off in regard to that issue and maybe also in regard to my emotions. I wanted to corner Dr. Marker and yell at him point blank, "Is he gonna make it? Is my son going to die??!!"

Torn

Dear Tommy,

    As I write, I realize Dad hasn't been mentioned so much. I guess initially for the first few months, you and I were pretty much partners alone in hospital survival. Your doctor dad's physical absence was due to the madhouse life of patients like you that he had to attend to at many other hospitals. So, we knew both sides—didn't we—as *we* drew energies and time from *your* attending physicians! Dad was with you in spirit through all that time and eventually was able to take off the last three weeks of your life. Thank God! Otherwise, that would have been a sore spot... for us as a couple—and as a family—and a horrible loss in his not being just a dad the last days of your life. Time was precious.

    A card I gave Dad in one of those dark times in February said, "Hello, morning—waking up with you is the nicest way to start any day!" Then I added, "Dear Mike, right now it has taken on a new angle of comfort... when words don't always describe or help, and numbness is often present. I love you! Jane."

Impending Separation

Dear Tommy,

Having you gone is so icky that I think we're only allowed split-second feelings of that true despair of this separation. It is so deep and intense.

There is an ongoing seepage of grief that I know will continue for the rest of our lives.

Even though I get so angry and scream at God and have told Him that He is mean and that I hate Him . . . I fall back into His embrace. Out of my pain, I feel even more charged up to reach out. And Christ *does* wish we were either cold or hot! Revelation 3:15.

The Gifts

Dear Tommy,

With cards, toys, stuffed animals, balloons, and candy that came for you, I hesitated to give you too many gifts in fear of spoiling you. But, the two I especially remember, made me glad I did.

One day you met me in the playroom, and as I handed you a single mylar balloon with a dinosaur on it, your face lit up and you embraced it as if I'd given you the world!

The other present was Big Bird. As soon as you saw the stuffed animal, you hugged it tight and rolled onto the bed with a sweet smile. Thanks was written all over you, and for a fleeting moment, the pain—the future and the past—went on hold, and my little guy was filled with joy from head to toe.

Thank You

Dear Tommy,

You know one thing that stands out in my mind about you? You'd always say "thank you." That's like the man in the Bible who had leprosy. We read about how he and nine other lepers were healed, but it was only one who came back to thank God for what he received. He remembered to say "thank you!" Ah, another one of those little kindnesses that is a grand percentage of life of love.

But, how does one say "thank you" to so many people who touched us in some way? There must be hundreds . . . through prayer, blood donations, smiles, hugs, cards, food, etc.

Tidbits

Dear Tommy,

    I remember all the balloons you got at a few times. It was almost embarrassing because I felt for those who didn't have any. You gave Nurse Pam a balloon, as well as a few others, but otherwise, you seemed proud that they were yours. In time, you couldn't even see a balloon any longer, so maybe these last bursts of color and love were stored up inside of you to keep you going in the darkness.

    —We began to guard time and triaged visitors.
    —Love from strangers (so neat!!)
    —Sex was hard during this time because the loss—the grief in your illness—was so intimate (I'd end up crying); sex felt almost sacrilegious.
    —So often on my drive home, I felt like I wanted to keep driving forever.

Loving Footprints

Dear Tommy,

It's neat how we were given a nurse named Faith. Her presence, like so many others, would leave a loving substance that continues to sustain us even after death—a reminder that the kingdom of God is within us... and we can all love each other and ourselves to the very fullest—in pain, in joy, in laughter, and in tears. It's a generosity without bounds.

Remember Peter from housekeeping, Tommy? He was a tall, slender fellow who was a favorite. Each morning his greeting acknowledged life itself—especially when he shared with me that he remembered you each night before he fell asleep. Peter became a rock to me—a reminder that *"The steadfast love of the Lord never ceases, His mercies never come to an end; they are new every morning; great is Thy faithfulness. 'The Lord is my portion,' says my soul, 'therefore, I will hope in Him'" (Lamentations, 3:22–24).*

Like one chaplain some years back told me, we are all "special specks." That's how God sees us. Each person is special to us in some way. Even if they presented a personality challenge—and my chemistry collided with theirs—it caused me to stand up to it with God in prayer. I had been asking to be less sensitive anyway, and these "obstacles" did help begin to give me the outer crust that I'd prayed for.

It blows my mind to think of all the people who have cared for you and touched you, Tommy, in three different hospitals. People of all ages, religions, nationalities, and personalities. All that divides us won't matter anymore once we're in heaven.

If those who can relate their deep love for you, Tommy, and then think of God's love for them—magnified and multiplied over and over... it is unimaginable!

Why should anyone be treated any less than anyone else? We are all children of a King!

To Be a Carrier

Dear Tommy,

Usually, I didn't dwell on the fact that I was a carrier of your disease. It was totally an unknown until you were born. One in a million children get this disease. Tommy, you, were the "chosen" one. Incredibly so, Dr. Paul Quie, the uncle of a good friend of ours was the expert in CGD at the University of Minnesota!

Then, to top it off, a friend from high school connected me with a friend of hers whose two boys have CGD, too! Small world! To say the least, I felt like I'd found a long lost friend in Cindi, and we tease each other about being "blood" sisters because we have the same genetic defect. How nice to be in company at such a time!

Well, if I didn't have the carrier state, maybe we'd be on our tenth child and Dad would be enrolled in Physicians Anonymous!

I remember one pediatrician long ago suggested in a gentle way that it must be hard to be a carrier. No one had ever approached me outside of Grandma and Grandpa in that way. It felt *so* good to be acknowledged and released that, yes, I do have some pain about being a part of the *cause* for your health troubles, Tommy. As a carrier, Grandma, too, felt responsible and hurt for us.

The "Steel Magnolias"

Dear Tommy,

One buoying force was a night out with a group of women friends we call "Steel Magnolias." Every few months or so, we would gather—six of us—Barb, Lois, Patti, Susie, Gail, and me. Each one enduring something that life had asked of her. In the understood given of darkness, we became listeners to one another and used "dinner out" time to let loose . . . gripe and toy with one of life's greatest weapons—humor. In the teasing and making light of our lives, an energy united created a strength—a steel in the rawness, in the tenderest of our emotions to move on "alone" in our separate journeys.

You were terribly sick the night I had an invitation to go out with the gals. I didn't want to, but Dad urged me to go, and I knew that I would be glad I went because it was ultimately for *both* you and me.

Gail has since died of cancer. We girls sent her roses that final week in the hospital. Each day one rose wilted. Then, Gail and the last rose died together on the same day.

Milestones

Dear Tommy,

To reassure your sisters was one thing. To try to reassure you about life seemed totally different. It felt so vague.

Your world was one of the unknowns—high temps, pain, nausea, and fighting with all your strength each day—bodily and all.

Kristin's and Maren's worlds were very affected by you, but it was not out of control in the same way. Kristin met me at the top of the stairs one night as I came home. She smiled telling me her period had started. Emergence as a woman. "Wow," I said hugging her, "How exciting!" But, she retorted quickly, "Well, it's not one of the Seven Wonders of the World either!"

And your big "normal" event, Tommy, was a lost tooth. But, it wasn't just an ordinary happy happening for me. It was strung with worry and questions like, "Will you be alive to lose any more?" I was thrilled that you had that experience.

At age nine, Maren was into reading "Garfield" and "On the Far Side." She announced that she had just begun shaving her legs . . . and dry, too! Ugh! And, Maren still loved to dismantle any mechanical-type item that was hers, or, seemed to be. Her curiosity was through and through.

Kristin's quick wit of "knowing it all" at age eleven made us laugh, didn't it? Her 'bookworm' ways with romantic teen novels and "Babysitter's Club" had ebbed now.

During your last four months at Children's Hospital, Dad's birthday, Kristin's and Maren's all came and went. So did Christmas, Valentine's Day, and Easter. We almost made it to your eighth birthday. Remember how we had planned to have your class of nine over? You suggested we divide it over two days so you could enjoy everyone and it wouldn't get too wild. Oh, how we laid that hope before us!

I promised you the trip, too, that you were next in line to

have alone with me. I remember the day when Maren and I got off the plane from Indiana. You grabbed my hand and said with a grin, "It's my turn next, Mom."

There's a tinge of feeling cheated in that time never coming around. But, then again, we had long hours of holding time in the hospital, even though you were sick and maybe in your earthly release. We are on a trip together—an inward-bound experience in the Spirit 'til that day we meet again, both as heavenly bodies.

It better be good!

Be Gentle on Yourself

Dear Tommy,

Time and again Dad and I raked ourselves over the coals for things we think we should have done—or could have done—for you. For a while, Dad made me give him a massage for each day that I knocked myself down with criticism. Needless to say, I was quite busy!

"Be gentle on yourself." Several people have consoled me with those words. That phrase hits my heart and fills me with a soft peacefulness.

I think back to young parenthood. Here's a portion of a letter I'd written to my parents some years back when Dad was in his sixth year of residency in California. I was six months pregnant with you. Maren was almost two and Kristin was three:

> One day last week was awful. I was at the peak of being out of control and tired of the demands of little ones. I was in tears, and suddenly Kristin and Maren were, too. Finally, deciding we were all stuck with each other at that moment, I sat in the rocker—one on each arm—and kept crying. I sang for a little bit in between, and Maren soon dozed off to sleep.
>
> Then, Kristin said, "I love you, Mommy." I responded, "I love you, too, Kristin." Then, she asked, "Do you love Maren?" (Yes, I do.) She smiled and said, "Do you love Daddy?" (Yes, I do.) She smiled again and then paused. *"Do you love yourself?"*

Those last words really hit deep. At that moment I didn't feel like I loved myself, but I told her I tried to love myself. Then, I thought about how Christ asks us to "Love your neighbor as yourself." I shared that with Kristin, and once again the impact of God's love for us and the worth that He gives us, is beyond imagination.

Intervention

Dear Tommy,

I had reached a point at which I felt like I couldn't love anyone but you. Maybe it was a time of switching gears and taking the plunge deeper spiritually and admit I had no control.

Kristin expressed, "I want you to be home more!"

Maren told me, "I hate you more and more. I'm resigning from the family. Get a new kid. I quit!"

One night a sign was attached to Maren's bed: "Mom, I don't want to talk to you."

That's when we asked for more help from the hospital's "Child Life" program. Christi became our mainstay helper, who had contact with you in art, reading, books, making milkshakes, and other activities while I had gone home for several hours at a time.

Christi took the girls under her wing. And as their friendship grew, she helped to be the objective person to listen to their feelings and help them see that the hospital vigil of a parent was no glamour job—it held the routine as any other job and I didn't always like it.

The girls and I began baking and decorating little cakes in the unit's kitchen, and in general we made more of an effort to do things together at the hospital as my need to be with you, Tommy, became more acute.

Then one day, as Maren and I sat in your room together in the rocker, with her arms about my neck, she moved her head squarely in front of me—eyes focused on mine—and softly said, "Mom, I think we're getting back together. There was a dark cloud over us."

Tommy, it was about that time that you said, "I wish I could be home three days without any pokes."

Maren was then aware that you did pay a high price in exchange for all the attention that you got as a sick kid. But, I understood her side, too. She, herself, had been chronically ill in all these years before, but nothing had been life-threatening. She had gotten pushed aside, in a way. We tried to build her up, too, along with Kristin, and verbalize what had been and what could lie ahead. They knew then that their littler brother was very sick and someday could die.

At some point, their many years of competing with you, Tommy—for time with me—changed. Allowed the feelings, they also became participants in play and in helping make you comfortable and feel loved.

It was obvious that along with the normal sibling rivalry—there was no one else who could take Kristin and Maren's place. You knew who your family was and loved it when all five of us were together. There was no earthly harmony quite like it.

A Choice

Dear Tommy,

One day when you began to look thinner, tired, and with dark circles under your eyes, I saw before me what had been my life calling...you! I had almost started a four-year nursing program, when true love (Daddy) lured me to the West Coast and we were married. Instead, I opted to be a mom at home shortly after. Little did I know that I would become your nurse. I used to entertain the idea of going back to school to become a nurse. You said, "Then you'd be helping everybody else. I want you to be just my nurse."

How could I resist such a request?! To the world, some would think that I tossed away—or lost a chance—to have a career. In my eyes, I had it all, and now even though you're gone, I still have you, Tommy...and maybe more so, in that spiritual teamship.

You told me, "Mommy, you're perfect because I love you." Thanks for loving me just as I am!

Cabin Fever

Dear Tommy,

I knew other people were aching so for you, too—family, friends, and hospital staff; people at home, school, church, the hospital . . . and even strangers had heard about your distress. It was a challenge to keep linked with people with ongoing new information and the roller-coaster ride that our emotions and faith were on.

In some ways, I didn't dare speak to too many about your condition, in that phobia-fear that it *would* get worse and you would die. Somehow by being guarded in that way, we thought we could protect you. Though maybe a silly thing, it gave us a tiny ounce of imagined control, if nothing else.

At times I felt jealous of Grandma being able to really talk and connect with our friends. I'd ask her to call a few people to keep them in touch with you. As deeply grateful as I was to my mom, I think I just longed to be the one to have the adult consolation and conversation with family and friends and share this crisis with them fully. In flashes I felt as if I was missing something, and yet my central focus was you. But as in all things, one burns out and grows weary. I couldn't be everywhere, with all, and run the show.

Ha! I remember one day when I was sitting on your hospital bed and said "Hi" to someone. You must have hit your tolerance level with me. You angrily protested, "Quit talking to everybody!"

One day I felt an intense feeling of being trapped, like claustrophobia in your now private room. I went out in the hall and saw Jerome the social worker. In those few moments of verbal exchange with Jerome, I felt renewed. I just needed out. Once back in the room, Dr. Marker came in and he saw my restlessness. It put me so at ease when he said he understood totally and related that he sometimes felt the same way—like the whole place was getting to him. At a later time, Dr. Marker did share that he had learned he wasn't indispensable as a physician. I, too, had come to grips with that for myself as a mom. Realistically, though, it was hard to make moments just for me— or with just the girls or Dad. I never missed a day with you, though, except for two days in the beginning when I had a bad cold. I fought any other sign of a cold successfully. The walls grew high, as did my immune system, to hold tight for the hard days ahead.

I often wonder how *you* did it, Tommy.

It must have been in March when you were so drained and weary of being awakened by nausea, vital sign checks, time for meds, and the general commotion of a unit and not being home, plus the worries that one so young shouldn't have to shoulder. You expressed to me, "I wish I could have some of that pizza medicine so I could get some sleep." (It was the kind they had used for you before surgeries for general anesthesia.)

"May you be made strong with all the strength which comes from His glorious power, so that you may be able to endure everything with patience" (Col. 1:11).

The Constant Observer

Dear Tommy,

Bone scan at 10:30. Waiting for tests, x-rays, and scans were all old hat for us both—but each time there was an anxiety because of what might be revealed. There was either a heave of relief of reassurance or some significant finding that showed up. Whatever, both did have their unknowns and made one ask, "What is it anyway?" It was hard to follow Christ's words of "Have no anxiety about anything." I have yet to succeed on that one!

We really lived hour by hour. It was impossible to go any other route because the scope of all you were going through was too complex and grandiose.

So eager for any information and wanting to know all the bits and pieces of your history, I'd open your chart now and then, unsure if that was really okay. I turned bright red one day when Dr. Belani walked in as you lay on the table for a scan as I thought, "Uh, oh—she caught me reading Tommy's chart."

It was no private thing though, I later found out—just that I was not allowed to write in it. Boy, was I tempted, though! I wanted them all to know what I felt and thought and observed, too. Sometimes all the vitals I'd done or physical signs I'd seen during blocks of hours at home didn't always get charted. Once in a while, I felt ignored. It was *me* who was the main observer every day for all these months. I was a constant. I was *your* MOM!

A Day of Reckoning

Dear Tommy,

Almost seven weeks had gone by and the fungal antibiotic wasn't working... and we had found out why.

Your particular aspergillus organism was resistant to the drug—amphotericin wasn't killing it.

Available on compassionate basis only was a drug called Itraconazole, that allowed an increase in cell membrane permeability and distributed well to tissues commonly involved in fungal infection. It was effective against aspergilli but was best when begun early on in the infection.

So, now that the organism was finally documented, the drug was released to us. I felt a mix of "Well, it's kinda late," but on the other hand, we needed to channel our hopes somewhere. The timing did seem miraculous in a way. The backup drug was visible to us as spectators and I felt that something was finally being done.

Surgery was now a possibility.

Psalm 91 was a good one at this time: *He who dwells in the shelter of the most high will rest in the shadow of the Almighty. I will say of the Lord, He is my refuge and my fortress, my God, in whom I trust.*

In the midst of all of this, we celebrated Cousin Michelle's 21st birthday in your room with a cake and candles that we had grabbed on the way to the hospital. To complete her special festivities, an entourage of nurses belted out "Happy Birthday!" And so, how ironic that Groundhog's Day should be a day of great joy for my godchild, Michelle, and yet for *her* godchild, you—Tommy, it was a day of reckoning. The groundhog must have been mixed up to see both sun and a blizzard.

Too Close to the Edge

Dear Tommy,

Probably one of the toughest days was when you began to cry out in pain about your eye. It looked red, and possibly something like conjunctivitis had set in.

Dr. Marker examined you, carefully checking out your eyes. Grandma (who was there, too, playing "Uno" with you and the girls earlier) held up an envelope over your left eye so that Dr. Marker could test your vision by holding up three, two, and then one finger.

At that moment, I think all of our hearts went into our throats. You couldn't see those fingers!!! It didn't take anyone to tell me that the organism had embedded itself elsewhere in your body.

Outside the door and out of earshot, Dr. Marker said to Daddy, "This organism is bad!" Together, they decided to summon Dr. Ramsay from the U and Dr. Carlson from Group Health.

Later on, we called Grandpa and Grandma back to the hospital along with the pastor. My voice broke both times and I cried, "I don't think he's going to make it."

Aunt Mary Lee came, too. We all ached along with each other in the panic of life slipping before our eyes. How much time did we have, anyway?

Mary Lee felt a sadness and had many feelings about the irony of not being a carrier and not wanting to have kids. I was a carrier and wanted ten kids.

Though skinny and pale, Tylenol and a bit of sleep had revived you. I wondered then if the hours before had all been a cruel joke. We didn't need the pastor. You looked okay to me. That hope and denial were to walk hand-in-hand with us the remainder of the time. From then on, it would be like Moses, whose arms had to be held up by others at a time of great distress.

God, too, had begun to carry us. We would, at times, ask Him to go a different direction, but the guy knew the whole picture. He knew a way out. The hard part was to trust that, as he carried us many times too close to the edge.

The whole spontaneous gathering with Pastor Rube turned into a celebration with you, Tommy, sending Grandma Doris into seventh heaven by wolfing down her turkey wild rice salad, which she had made and brought to the hospital for you—a favorite of yours! You were a bit dismayed that we were going to lay hands on you, but Rube promised we would be finished for 6:00—in a few minutes—for a Disney program.

Thank God for Kleenex

Dear Tommy,

Surgery was set for Thursday, February 8 at 12:30 P.M. You were to have a thoracotomy to de-bulk the mass attached to your heart sac and lung. They would put in a new port-a-cath as well, in the chance that there was fungal growth there.

On February 6, in the last ditch efforts on the pioneering front of this monster organism, you received your first white cell transfusion that evening. It would at least make an attempt to help enable your body to put up a fight. There were side effects of white cell transfusions, but you adapted well and received them most nights from then on. To think of the web of people—family, medical staff, and other friends and strangers who would donate blood to team up with you in this fight, amazed me. The risk of unknowns in blood giving seemed comparably small in contrast to the love that even made this service possible.

In time, one woman from War Memorial Blood Bank would call us at the hospital to check on you, Tommy. The attachments to you and to all of us who, as a team, tried to save you felt like the best of communities.

I remember one of your first MRI scans. They had to check out your head, too. Despite being slightly sedated, you panicked when the helmet part was put on your head. You pushed it off and exclaimed, "I feel trapped!" So, sedated again, you pretty much slept through the test as I reassured you over and over again that it would be okay. And, of all the people who should talk—I'm "Ms. Claustrophobia," herself! Your little red tape recorder equipped with music tapes that we had brought to every x-ray and scan was overpowered by the loud, fragmented hum of the MRI. Deep inside the narrow tunnel, you looked swallowed up in a dark invisible capsule that once again I felt almost unable to penetrate. (Pancreatitis didn't help in the scan.)

Patti, a nurse who had accompanied me that day to the scan was a welcome partner to talk with and distracted my mind from the wait and the worry. Dad joined us, too. I always felt a comfort when he was present.

As Dad and I played a game of pool with you on fifth floor two days before surgery, you began to shake and spike a fever. As we were about to head back to our home unit—fourth floor—Dr. Marker broke the news to us of the MRI results. Three lesions had showed up on the brain.

Back in our room, Dad and I pulled the curtain around the three of us. It seemed darker than usual.

Suddenly, it seemed sick everywhere—germs, clutter, and stuffiness. Perturbed with too many Kleenex boxes in the room, I angrily piled them on the night stand. But God saw ahead. We began to cry as you dozed and were hooked up to who-knows-what medicine. Kleenex by Kleenex, we let it out. And do you know the "damn too many Kleenex boxes" were used, one by one.

An abscess on the kidney, an eye mass, and three lesions on your brain. Which do you worry about? Blindness, a morphine addiction, you entering a vegetative state? Our thoughts were more on the whole picture of life itself.

After Midnight

Dear Tommy,

I promised that I would sleep in your bed the next night. You were excited! The least I could give you—it felt like the only thing, and yet even though you were facing blindness and death, your priority and concern was to have someone to play with you; to be cuddled and to be comforted.

One night at home, I couldn't fall asleep. My body had energy that I had never felt before. It was after midnight and as I lay in bed, the horror hit me. It was a split-second glimpse of the deep grief I felt. Dad was sound asleep, so I went in your empty room to plug in our phone, sat on the floor and dialed 4 East.

Who should answer but Patti who had been with me during the MRI brain scan! She had time to talk, and in her warm ways, she listened as I felt safe to pour out my fears and my tears about our little boy. Wrapped in a blanket, I sobbed and unbottled my insides. Then, I began to shake uncontrollably and cried more. Patti's healing extended care was to all of us—not just to you, Tommy, as she said, "We care more than we want to sometimes."

Through her I felt surrounded by God and collapsed into a much needed sleep alongside Daddy. I knew he was hurting, too, but he had to get up early to face another day of dealing with surgeries and patients while you hung heavy over it all.

Privacy

Dear Tommy,

Moved to a private room now, you had a better stab at being able to get some shut-eye. Privacy was a tough element to come by anyway with all the interruptions, so this was a positive step. We had been there almost two months, so I guess seniority and illness put in their dibs.

Family was so good to swing by—just often enough not to become pests.

Uncle Tom and his girlfriend, Sue, stopped by that evening before lung surgery. Their presence helped ward off some anxiety and put a hand of familiarity out toward the world of unknowns. It's like being eight to nine months pregnant—you have no choice. You know you have to give birth to that child inside soon. It's going to come and you can't stop it.

Round-the-Clock Reassurances

Dear Tommy,

Your Scripture verses in school for February and March were Psalm 23:1–6. To hear those words and yet actually be putting them into your life for real must have been both scary and a comfort-like verse four: *Even though I walk through the valley of the shadow of death, I fear no evil; for Thou art with me; Thy rod and Thy staff they comfort me.*

And how timely that the month you died, April's verse was John 3:16: *For God so loved the world that He gave His only Son, that whoever believes in Him should not perish but have eternal life.* Wild, eh?!

*   *   *

Letters and cards to all of us were like food. Often we'd open the mail late at night and feel a warm breeze float through our souls as we "heard" the voices express love and concern.

Phone calls were that way, too, but demands on time from so many directions made that type of communication tough, especially relating the story over and over again. Notes were less intrusive.

One bitsy note that my mom wrote is another I carried in my purse and re-read. It reminded me of who was really in charge and who the greatest Physician was:

February 20, 1990
"Dear Jane, *'I am holding you by your right hand . . . I, the Lord our God . . . and I say to you, don't be afraid, I am here to help you" (Isaiah 41:13).*
"I love you! Mom"

At one point, a friend's overseas letter ministered to me in a similar way. It was a goose-bumping, comforting feeling when she said she awoke seven hours earlier in Belgium and began praying as we fell asleep! Wow! Round-the-clock prayer from everywhere! Some we knew in China, Sweden, California, etc., were in on it, too.

Holli ended with John 14:27: *"Peace I leave with you; my peace I give to you. I do not give to you as the world gives. Do not let your hearts be troubled and do not be afraid.* Thinking and praying for you all daily."

Crossword Puzzles, Fishing, and Peanut M&M's

Dear Tommy,

Can you believe that you had a surgeon who was Neil Diamond's look-a-like? What with our being Neil Diamond fans, this guy had a head start in our trust. Two and a half years ago, Dr. Roback had done a thoracotomy on you. He was about to do the same thing once again. It had taken several months to recoup from that aspergillus.

Going into induction—the room where they initiate sleep before surgery (anesthesia)—was one of the toughest parts for me. I think that's because we would watch you go under. You would become limp and then look dead. It's like the mind gets tricked. There's such relief when we see you again after surgery and you give that first indication of movement and response.

About three and a half hours later, the shell of the mass had been cleaned out and drained. A slight residue was left on the heart, but we hoped the Itraconazole would resolve that.

Who should you have as your first nurse in the Life Support Unit but your first grade classmate Chris's mom, Kathy! As He had done and would do time and again, the Holy Spirit connected us to His continual presence through so many avenues of people and events.

So, there you were under bright lights with a new port-a-cath, a fresh incision, drainage tubes, and those other lines that miraculously enable life to continue a gift of healing, or lessen pain—blood, antibiotics, the works! The sight of you sprawled out in the flesh with a respirator was overwhelming. I hugged Kathy and cried. Daddy was teary eyed, too, as we took your hands gently into ours and reassured you of our presence and of our love. (We weren't sure at first *where* to touch!)

Daddy found a wonderful distraction from the intensity of life surrounding us—crossword puzzles! I must admit they must have been a saving grace to focus in on, but I would get annoyed once in a while if I needed to talk while he was working on one. He could get *really* absorbed in another world! But, that is a gift that is an asset to Dad as a surgeon. I would want someone with good concentration if I was operated on!

As the hours ticked by, we were so glad, as I know you sure were, to have your respirator removed. Ah, to hear your first words, "ICE CHIPS." It was a glorious sound.

Having male nurses was a neat change for you, it seemed. Kevin was such a honey. As Grandma wrote in her journal:

> Kevin was his nurse on my day, and what a fine, caring, attentive fellow. Tommy is always so cooperative and wants to know what's happening play-by-play. The difficult time was the med tech, giving him a finger prick to draw blood—many times—and the blood seemed to clot on her. It was most difficult to hear Tommy cry out, "Is that the last one?" And I knew there would be more. After a brief rest, Kevin came with a needle to check on drawing blood from his arm. He talked so quietly and reassuring to Tommy and decided he had a good vein, and Tommy hardly knew the needle had gone in.
>
> I held his hand most of the time and occasionally rubbed his leg. I could feel the nodules on his leg. Tommy continues to have pain in the abdomen and that comes in waves.

Dealing with your pain at this point was a bit bewildering. You were put on a PCA (Pain Control Anesthesia) pump so that you could be the master of the medicine and give yourself, within prescribed bounds, how much you needed. There was a little button near your hand that you could push to release the morphine. It seemed odd to see your chubby little hand, so young, having to be at the mercy of disease and pain. It wasn't fair . . . nor were we promised on this earth that it would be.

The surgeon took away much of your pain medicine with the idea that you would move more and facilitate healing. We watched the reverse happen. You hurt more and more so you would guard your wound. It was a tough lesson to learn, and we became advocates for administering pain meds. No one is going to overdose! The nurses were fun to watch on this. They were covetous of their patients and aggressive when they needed to tell the doctors to up the pain dosage. I guess a nurse doesn't work one-on-one with a patient for twelve hours at a stretch and not be in harmony with a person's needs and emotions. If they're not, it's a cruel spot for the patient to be in.

I remember Kevin promising you a fishing day with him in the near future when you got better. We hung onto that future. Anything we could plant out there as a hope or a "lure"—some goal—we'd do it.

It's like Bruce in the x-ray department. After some surgeries in the months ahead, I jokingly promised that you and I would bring him a bag of peanut M&M's in the summer—a treat-love of his. As it turned out, you didn't go fishing with Kevin. And Bruce got his pound of peanut M&M's, but I went alone.

Leg Rubs

Dear Tommy,

It took five days to get back up to 4 East from the Life Support Unit, but we made it, didn't we? Exposed to chicken pox by a hospital worker, you were put in a special room with double doors. It felt so isolated and yet a momentary welcome from the action-packed LSU.

Sometimes I wondered if the ache and pain in your legs wasn't from the fungus nodules alone, but from the stress and tension building inside from the unknowns and being cooped up for so long.

I remember spending hours rubbing your legs as we would listen to tapes by Dr. Roxanne Daleo—some called "Mindworks for Children." They were tapes that we were introduced to during a rough year you had coping with needle pokes. They helped you image and relax. You were a pro at it and clung to one of the phrases: "I can do what I say I can. I can do it; yes, I can!"

Love Notes

Dear Tommy,

Valentine's Day. I remember buying pink paper and crayons and candy sticks for you to work on for your nine classmates. Weeks before, at one point, you had the energy to make *one*. It was for Angela . . . a valentine that I handed to her at your funeral. What a lucky little lady!

Your dear first grade teacher, Mrs. Szwaja, helped open the lines of communication with the happenings in your class as had Mrs. Henderson the year before, when you spent some of kindergarten at home.

Mrs. Szwaja wrote to Dad and me, "This bag has Tommy's valentines and his treats. Also, we had awards for the most stars. Tommy won second place. So, he gets the bike sticker."

These touches of love were extended by so many. It was a community of love that breathed into us the strength and hope we needed to simply "wait on the Lord." As our priest friend, Brian, would later write after your death (referring to when he and I were on an internship together at Loma Linda Hospital), "I do vividly remember the strong atmosphere of Christian love that dominated a hospital filled with pain and struggle each day. Eventually, with the healing of time and strong faith, there were always signs of new life. I will pray for these signs for you all."

Lost and Found

Dear Tommy,

Dropping a full pop can on my toe almost drove me to the ceiling and to a new vocabulary. In seconds, I thought of how are you handling your abdominal pain?! It must be hell.

More tests to probe that pain in nuclear medicine put us into the hands of Dr. Murray—the surgeon who performed your next surgery on February 16, barely one week after lung surgery.

Inserting a needle into the liver showed the narrowing of the head of the pancreas. The pathway from the liver to the small intestine was so obstructed and caused back pressure and pain. The gall bladder was the recipient of that pressure, so a tube was attached to a catheter outside your body to drain the fluid buildup. It seemed to do the trick, along with the morphine. (Itraconozale again.)

Before you went into this surgery, I felt so alone. Dad wasn't able to be there at that time. He was working, trying to be physician to many, and yet, too, a dad of a very sick patient—his son.

This surgery took place next door to Children's Hospital at Abbott Northwestern. The hospital was unfamiliar, and their routines didn't correlate with that total focus on children. And so, as much as I wanted to stick by your side, I wasn't assertive enough to ask if I could somehow keep you with me until they were ready for you. Instead, we parted with a kiss and an uncomfortable feeling of letting you go. Did you feel that way? Before surgery, it is *so* crucial for parent and child to say "good-bye" and feel good about it. There's always that lurking wonderment that risk involves. You never know if it's the end. You never know for sure if your child will come out of surgery alive.

I felt lost as to where to wait. I wanted to be sure the doctor could find me. Perhaps all the anxiety from the past two months culminated in that moment, but I began to cry and paged Dad. Who should show up but your cousin and godmother, Michelle! She calmed me down with her concern and with simply who she was to me. She had always been like my kid, and now she was twenty-one! We waited this one out together.

Dad was able to come by as you finished in surgery. Just hearing they were almost done made me feel great joy. That fear of losing you, of being on the edge was ever present—it has always been that way with a chronic illness—but the reality sat boldly before us now.

We all gathered in a room with Dr. Murray to review the past two hours hidden from us. I remember when I first met Dr. Murray—the kind eyes and beard he had—like those Old/New Testament films . . . real Christ-like.

And I think that's what drew me to so many. Christ was there continually reaching out in each person who was present.

Dr. Stafford and Dr. Marker were there, too—all so hoping the cure for your tummy pain was resolved.

I felt so deeply for the frustration and struggle the doctors all must have had in dealing with finding answers and healing you. I verbalized this to Dr. Marker, and he said they wrestled with it as we parents do. I knew he understood. Words couldn't have expressed any more. I felt a teamship; a bond.

The Rubber Banana

Dear Tommy,

I have a tendency to put everyone on a pedestal, but as my tears began to flow a little more and I let people see my fears and my vulnerability, humanity itself came more alive and embraced us in new ways.

One day when Dr. Belani came by, she leaned against the door frame and said, "If we didn't have kids like Tommy, we'd be walking around with halos on our heads." I could feel her compassion and her desire to make you well, Tommy. She loved you so much.

I remember running into Kiran on the way back from lunch one day, and she grabbed my arm to wait. As we paused, she pulled out a little two-inch rubber yellow banana! I used to bring you bananas with ribbons on them to encourage your potassium intake at one time, and here was a little light humor that reached deep into my heart. It was Dr. Belani's way of expressing her concern and love. It was a touch of healing—the type that I gravitated to more and more as we knew you may not be healed in any earthly way, the way your physicians hoped would happen.

A Pause in the Hall

Dear Tommy,

I always liked when Dr. Marker sat down and talked a few minutes. In his ways, he helped me believe in myself and in my care for you, Tommy, and in the encouragement of our situation. His presence was a comfort.

Remember how he would start to come in every time you were on the bedpan during those periods of diarrhea? What timing! It was worth the laughter, though—maybe not for you, but I needed it.

Dr. Glasser stopped me in the hall one day as you had a wagon ride. His touch on my shoulder was so appreciated. His words conveyed his knowing of the severity of your situation and that we were fortunate to have had seven years with you. He made me confront the crisis. On one hand, I felt a defense at the abrupt fact, and on the other hand, I felt a great wash of love. It must not be easy for others to reach out to touch such pain. But, I knew that they, too, felt it.

Counting to Infinity

Dear Tommy,

If nothing else, I was glad you had a solid grasp on God. You knew that you could talk to Him *any* time of the day or night. He was the pivotal position to have to meet any challenge. You weren't alone. It's like Dad's picture he had as a youth and that was on your wall—of Christ behind the young man at the helm of a ship. He was with you in the storms and in the stillness.

I remember at five years old your telling us, "Jesus is the only one who can count to infinity." That sums up our knowledge of Him, doesn't it? We must trust in His boundless love and His ways.

With an eye surgery (vitrectomy) scheduled for February 20, we, too, had to trust God in a deeper way than we ever had. (Vitrectomy involves removing the vitreous substance and with a saline solution injecting amphotericin.)

At this time, I knew I had experienced a peace. But, I was angry that you were going through pain, Tommy. There were so many systems involved.

I flashed back to the dream that I had when I was pregnant with you—that you would have a health problem, but to be at peace because God's hand was on you. I knew something was bodily wrong and that there was a bigger picture. At that point I felt that faith, endurance, and hope in my life made it easier to deal with. I thought I could accept your death, but I knew it would be awful (I'll say it is!). Like friend Elsie told me years after her husband died of cancer: "Don't even *try* to imagine death. You can't!"

The Healing Issue

Dear Tommy,

Probably the hardest thing to cope with was the issue of your healing. There are several interpretations of it. The one that created a spiritual judgment feeling in Dad's and my heart was the one in which if you don't have faith, healing won't come—the idea of unbelief not facilitating a promise of healing.

It's hard to even share this because in my view, in my defense, I would never want to mislead anyone or wrong God.

But you died, Tommy, and you had the faith to move mountains. That, I don't doubt. I believe that from the time of your being in my womb, God was telling us through several dreams that something would be very wrong with your health, but to be at peace—His hand was on you.

I think when certain healing tapes and pamphlets and requests to lay hands on you by people whom we didn't know came our way, Dad and I felt confused...not that anyone intended to hurt us, though.

I am kind of lost as to what we can, or if there *is* anything we can, command God to do. My whole theology of God encompasses His love. It seems to limit Him by making any other doctrines and all. It seems wrong. He's sovereign—the supreme authority (Isa. 55:8–9):

> For my thoughts are not your thoughts,
> Neither are your ways my ways says the Lord.
> For as the heavens are higher than the earth,
> So are my ways higher than your ways
> And my thoughts than your thoughts.

Watching the world of medicine, one sees so many limitations. As many miracles that there are within, there's a spiritual realm that rises far beyond *and* far within, too—where the Kingdom of God is.

I believe in earthly-physical healing. God does heal, though not always earthly. Maybe I didn't feel strongly enough about you being healed here on this earth. Perhaps I didn't stand hard enough in prayer against, as some would say, "the attack" or the "battle" of disease.

You prayed to be well. You had told me that you wished it was two years before when you were a lot healthier and running around. You also told me that you were glad you were the youngest, because the youngest die last. Then you added, "Well, usually."

I felt a great calm and peace when Pastor Valen prayed one Sunday at church in regard to those who are sick—that healing will come either way, whether here physically or in heaven. I wanted you *fully* well and I also remember thinking that heaven was an option that I felt ready for.

My tears have come often, Tommy, since you died in wondering if I could have prevented your death somehow...in feeling that I felt or did something wicked.

The emotions are very real and it is scary how condemned one can feel through certain places of worship or amid varying beliefs of people.

But, we walked through this fire journey, and it wasn't alone.

When relating my anguish years later to friend Brenda about this healing issue, she simply told me, "Jane, you loved Tommy so much that you prayed for the end of his suffering."

The Huddle

Dear Tommy,

Your sister, Maren (nine years old at the time) asked me point blank one day before that eye surgery, "How much money is in my savings? I would like to put it all toward Tommy." Ah, a child's heart!

Backtracking—the day before your vitrectomy, I remember how you reveled in Spaghetti-O's. I even saved a menu because your precious handwriting often added that particular entrée next to the options listed for that day. As you talked with one of your good buddies by phone, I heard you tell Tim, "They say I'm getting better." I wondered if you really believed it yourself, Tommy. I guess we had to believe it to fuel our energy for the good fight, eh?

That day before the eye surgery was the day when we realized that you were very possibly going to be blind. It was the day, too, that our eyes opened to another world—a world where our eyes and our hearts had to fully turn and rest in God, or we would go nuts.

Remember after those special pre-surgery drops were put into your eye, Dad and I sat with you? In a despairing cry, you said, "I feel like I'm blind. This is the worst time of my life!"

"It's scary, isn't it?" I said. "We feel scared and panicky, too, Tommy." Then, we three just huddled together and cried a long time. None of us could protect the other.

"Where two or three are gathered in my name, there I am in the midst of them," says Christ. He, too, was in that huddle.

My eyes wandered to your baby photo album on the bed that I had brought that day. Frantic, I knew that maybe this was the last day you could look at it. I had a need for you to see it earlier on, but I respected your disinterest and lack of energy to look. I wished then that I had spent even more time doing some of these things. They were more high expectations I guess I had of myself to do with you kids. But it didn't matter anymore. It was maybe too late now. Our hearts sank deep. The reality of that barrier overwhelmed Dad and me. It was some kind of horror that was all too quickly robbing us . . . of something that was so familiar to our day—*to be able to see*, that until it slips away, you don't see that you took it so for granted.

You know your little friend, Christopher Strommen, who is blind as a consequence of being born too early? Well, his dad reached out to Daddy with a neat message. Jim wrote:

Dear Mike,

I just thought I would drop you a card to say we are thinking about you. It's no revelation to say there is something special about father-son. We'll always have our sons, even if we are temporarily separated from them by death or other curtain. Give me a call sometime.

In Christ,
Jim

The Little Things

Dear Tommy,

    The eye mass had grown quickly since the MRI and the little lesions had begun in the other eye. Would it ever stop? Where were we headed anyway? How would it affect you/us?

    Eyesight was so precious, and life even more so... but somehow the eyesight was a tangible substance for me as spectator, and an easier thing to grieve over because life itself was incomprehensible to lose. But in possibly letting go of that eyesight, we were losing part of you... and yet in a way, heaven became nearer. Its company wasn't so bad.

    In fact, maybe I even wondered why we clung so to this world. In the gloom—and in seeming to sink so low—I got a wee glimpse of something much better. I couldn't touch it in the way I wanted (maybe because it touched me?), but it came in the little things... in joy, in faith, in hope, in love. And, love must not be so little after all.

A Fear

Dear Tommy,

It's funny the fears we conjure up. And yet the feelings are there and valid. During your hospitalization I had an onset of an intermittent crinkly sound in my left ear. As it continued, I thought, 'What if I go deaf and Tommy is blind?' What communication is really left? Our worlds could be sealed shut to one another.

Stark Realities

Dear Tommy,

You took your eye patch off the evening of February 22. My heart raced into my throat as you asked for a mirror. I'm not sure what you expected or what you saw, but you had apparently faced that fear and were silent for a while. Then, you seemed satisfied to move on. You could see light and dark with that eye. The other was okay, but the lesions there were growing, too.

By the next day, Tommy, your pains were less and you seemed interested in food again. You slept so much, but I suppose you needed to catch up after a month or more of nausea and stomach pains.

On this very day, Grandma took your Great-grandpa Elmer to Midway Hospital for an echocardiogram and an aorta ultrasound—similar tests to yours, Tommy. You and your buddy, Grandpa Elmer! I learned from Grandma how excited she was to pick you and me up at Children's Hospital to take us to "3312"—home! She saw you there waiting with Nurse Ann and noted how tentatively you walked to the car with your gall bladder bag or discharge at your side. With a patch on one eye and the other eye closed, you seemed quite comfy in the back seat. You weren't too talkative with Grandma while I popped into a yogurt store, except you answered her question that you had to return at 5:00.

It was this day at home that you suddenly looked like an old man, Tommy—bile bag in one hand and other arm on the rail, ever so slowly putting one foot ahead of the other with great effort up the stairs. Those once strong shoulders had grown weary and burdensome. They suddenly looked so tiny, so soft, so very tender; so very tired. I'd come to know your body better than my own. You headed for Nintendo and with one eye still functioning, you played briefly. My worry was that you might wear yourself out. I felt torn and bad that I had even confronted you about it. I'm sorry I sounded so cross. I hurt your feelings, I think. I knew it was a perfectly good escape for you from your illness, and I believe it provided a boost and testing ground to your abilities and limitations at that point. You kept challenging yourself in different ways. Your dignity hung in a fragile balance.

Typically on these passes home, you would head for our bed, often in my arms because you couldn't make it up the last flight of stairs.

It was at home that the stark reality of your weakened state hit me hardest. I was used to a high-powered mover of a boy whose movements were ever so purposeful but loaded with energy, laughter, and response to life; to people.

You had no interest in your own bedroom anymore and we grieved that absence—a change that only intensified our missing you at home. We almost forgot at times what it was like to have you home. And yet, we hauntingly would expect you to peek around the corner or call us to come lie by you the many weeks and weeks and weeks you were in the hospital.

It delighted us that you chose our bed as *the* place to retreat to. Symbolically, your room stood empty, but even in your disease and sickness, our room was oh, so full of you! Sometimes I was content to just do things around the house and catch up with laundry and all else and check on you now and then as you slept. Sometimes I'd hold you on the bed in the pillows and just sit and be silent as you dozed. That space away from everyone, even though you slept most of the time, was a sacred haven—a harbor of safety from needles and the run of people who took care of you. Those passes home helped you catch your breath, and you knew, too, that there y*ou* had the control. You were free from interruptions, free from being a guest—as homes should be; a place to be free to let go.

The Lost Lizard

Dear Tommy,

Toward the end of February, I remember thinking things must be better. There had been fewer tears, and Daddy no longer expressed his wish to just be a dog!

Maren's animal menagerie at home channeled us into a healthy detour at times. You are well aware of the high percentage rate of escapism that her pets tend to have, yes? Like her huge frog I found in my closet one morning, and the night one of her bunnies escaped and Dad was on his hands and knees hunting for it at 2:00 A.M.! Well, it happened *again*! One evening we got home from the hospital, and we discovered her newt had disappeared. We all took a room and hunted. What a great mind diversion *and*, too, attention that Maren no doubt needed. Logic finally had us check the humidfier again, and lo and behold, the newt was there . . . lovingly taken into the arms of your puffy-eyed sister who had cried so hard that it almost seemed like overkill.

I knew she was devoted to her pets to the point once of even having me close her windows, despite her discomfort in the summer heat, so that her new tadpoles would grow faster.

The lost lizard helped trigger tears that needed to come. Maren was losing you, Tommy, her brother and her friend.

Laughter

Dear Tommy,

Back at Children's Hospital that night during TV's "Family Matters," you smiled and laughed. It had been weeks since a smile had appeared, and it seemed to take the edge off all of us. What a celebration in such a simple thing! Oh, it was a highlight of the month . . . if not *the* highlight!

You seemed rested and peaceful as you prayed, Tommy. I remember after you asked the Lord many times to help you get well, you seemed to want to assure me with, "Sometimes it takes some people a very long time to get well."

I hoped that little head of yours wasn't full of some twisted guilt for not being healed. You had asked at one point about the IV pump—if it was evil or the devil. I said no, that it was good—an avenue to help get medicine into you and to make you well.

At this point, the three lesions on the brain looked smaller. But, your temperature continued.

Shootin' the Breeze

Dear Tommy,

Grandpa Roland and Grandma Doris pitched in with keeping you company at times so that the girls and I, or Dad and I could grab some "time off," so to speak.

One day when Grandpa and Aunt Mary Lee were there, they read to you and talked, etc. Sounds like you seemed quite interested in Mary Lee's move to a new apartment. I bet Grandpa told you some jokes or showed you some neat tricks. He always had some fun thing up his sleeve... you were guaranteed not to be bored!

And you and Grandma had some rip-roarin' competitive "Uno" games, I hear, while we were out. Was she a good sport? Your enthusiasm helped her spirits, too.

The Basketball

Dear Tommy,

Two and a half months had passed in the hospital, and my promise in January that we would go home soon made me feel like a liar. The passes home helped ease that somewhat.

After being home on pass one day right before the dreaded return to the hospital, Grandpa and Grandma brought over a basketball signed by all the St. Louis Park girls' team members. Your former babysitter, Jill, was on that team. This gift was especially for you. Remember they had dedicated at least one basketball game to you, Tommy?!

Your first reaction was to cry . . . amidst all the noise of oohs and aahs that Kristin and Maren and we were expressing. But, you were obviously happy about the basketball and gingerly got off your kitchen chair and showed a burst of energy, dribbling the ball a few steps. You wanted it with you at the hospital, contrary to what we thought.

Shots

Dear Tommy,

The effectiveness of Itraconazole at this point was an unknown. The fungus was insidious—that means that it had an uncertain and possibly more dangerous nature than was evident, and it takes quite a while for any results to show.

Barraged at this point with several antibiotics and antibacterials, plus white cell transfusions, and IV foods (no "Fun Fruits!"), they decided to add good ol' interferon.

Given by intermuscular shot, this drummed up a whole new set of emotions. Daily blood draws were enough, weren't they?

My mind flashed back several years to your hate of needles. At about age five or six, you said, "I wish I was a puppet; then, I don't have to have shots," and "I'm gonna steal all the prick needles and butterflies and throw them away and break them." "Does the hospital have sharp needles? Are they clean?" And in regard to your weariness of doctor appointments, you said, "I wish it was in infinity days—then we'd be done."

Anyway, so the order had been given to take interferon. It would have to be taken after the white cell count to keep close watch on fever reaction, etc. I don't even know how they could tell. You were on so much stuff and so sick.

So, the timing of it had to be late at night, and I know you worried so about it. Thank God you weren't on the shots for long. We told you to call us *anytime*, so we could be with you, at least by phone, reassuring you. We had to trust that the nurses would honor that.

A couple of the nurses even offered to let me give them practice shots in the stomach or thigh to enable me to master the technique for whatever the future brought us to ... home-care and who knew? The gesture itself of me poking these gals made me feel closer to them than ever; like old college buddies. They really cared! I think we were all so nervous for you, Tommy, and wanted to make things as okay as possible, that we united in a type of sisterhood in that effort.

Reminding you about my childhood friend, Stephanie, helped. She is a diabetic and has had to give herself shots for years. You knew Stephanie and drew comfort in that camaraderie and told me to *be sure* to tell her of your first shot. You knew that she personally understood. She knew that it was a big deal. After tucking you in at the hospital, I called Stephanie the minute I got home.

Compassionate Community

Dear Tommy,

One of the most awesome things for me to feel and watch in this whole four-month segment was the unfolding and building of community. I think community is always there, but there are times in your life when you have to make it happen or you have a choice to be apart; *and* there are times when community comes to you.

I think, too, that there are some people who are very open to letting others in and responding. But also, even if there are certain people—both parents and medical staff who can't receive or reach out in love—it doesn't mean the appreciation or impact is any less. One-sided giving is tough, but people do change and one can't underestimate their own love as seed-planting for the future.

For me, the hospital became what I envision as the ultimate church. It's like in being a mom at home. I was fortunate to be able to do that and believed strongly in what I was doing. Likewise, if you believe in God the Father, God the Son, and God the Holy Spirit, you need a place of support to keep encouraging you, like church.

So, in *this* place at Children's Hospital, where our war with darkness took place, kindness became the supportive friendship in itself that lifted us to higher ground—to where the invisible was most powerful—where God was ever present.

I believe that the key to this medical community of compassion was that they dared touch our pain over and over again. As hard as it was—as much as they try to shield themselves from burn-out and crossing professional lines—they suffered, too. It takes a lot of love and warmth to keep someone warm when they are dying. It takes a lot of love and warmth by many when tears are leaking out all over at the hospital, at your school, Tommy, at our church, and among family and friends here at home and faraway.

The social worker continued to encourage Dad and me to think of us, too, and give adequate care to ourselves. Considering the circumstances, we took heed of his words and got out once in a while. But ever more powerful was the fact that he shed light on that need and that he recognized it was there and cared.

Jerome's ministry to the nurses must have been behind closed doors, out of earshot, as they, too, needed to talk about their charges and dilute feelings as well. The intense care for their young patients—which roamed also to patient family members at times—was a wide-range job that encompassed many roles... especially if a parent wasn't present.

I could think of *each* person who cared for you, Tommy, or who smiled or said "hi" in the stairwell or who mopped your room, or who silently shared their concern with their eyes, with their tears. I could tell you what was special about them and how they touched me in their own unique way.

Each nurse, each doctor, each employee had their own gifts; their own way of connecting and relating.

I think back on Kelly, one of your nurses on 4 East. We would laugh so when I'd return from lunch because she had a thing for tidying up and wanting things spic and span and in their place. You had so much junk piled up in your room, Tommy, that her clean-ups gave such a calm and momentary space of order, of control. It was only months later that summer that her life would be turned upside down. Her boyfriend, Scott, was killed instantly in a motorcycle accident. What sorrow! I never dreamed I'd be crying for Kelly. However heaven works, perhaps you and Scott have met and in some way you guys have been a part of healing in our lives... in making new spaces for God to do good.

Broken—Dr. Reaney

Dear Tommy,

"Do unto others as you would have them do unto you; love others as yourself." My mind flashes back to a time when the girls brought home designs for making buttons at school with the theme, "Others before self." I just about lost it. I wanted to scream and rant and rave. True—there are many times when life is just that: "others before self," but we also need to know our own situation. And in the chronic illness shadow—as in the hospital month of March 1990—I knew I had to pace myself and in my heart, go away to pray as Christ did. I was on empty.

March 6th you seemed to be turning a corner. Then, on March 8th, things changed. You began to feel with more intensity a burning sensation—a pain in your fingers and toes.

A cartoon from *In-Fisherman* magazine that Daddy passed my way depicted my feelings at that point. It showed a group of fifteen inexperienced tourist muskie fishermen squished in a boat together, "All simultaneously slinging two-pound razor-sharp, multi-hooked lures."

It was a time when a doctor would enter your room, and I wasn't sure which body part it was for! That was the setting in which Dr. Jud Reaney came into our lives. A pediatric physician who dealt in pain control, I was eager to have someone for you who could zero in on you and be a cheering person; another advocate for you who could head-on meet the worst enemy for you at this point . . . pain.

I knew you had had it, Tommy, when buddy Kyle came to visit one day with his mom. You were struggling to be a host. Usually delighted with his presence, you seemed agitated with Kyle's endless energy. Perhaps combined with the pain, you were angry that you couldn't interact with Kyle like good ol' times. Kyle and his mom left after not too long, but they got a glimpse of your world and in a way, it helped me not to feel so isolated. They became aware of your high point of pain and frustration.

So, when Dr. Reaney walked in, I wished he had walked right back out! You and I were both so cranky and tired. I wasn't ready for this new bout with pain. You needed a rest. So did I. Dr. Reaney interviewed us both as to your history and your latest development with pain that both of us hardly knew about. It was obvious that you had me wound around your finger and we were both out of control. He confronted you as to your bossing me around and me letting you. All I felt was that Dr. Reaney was attacking us—that he didn't know our world and how hard we had fought. I needed someone to tell me something good. I didn't feel like starting over with *another* person—another person that would ask for your time and interrupt us and be a bother. I didn't want him to see me so vulnerable.

And yet, here he was and I had pushed for his services.

In Dr. Reaney's soft-spoken manner, he began to win us over, despite the strikes that that day had put against him. It was a day that we both broke, Tommy, and it was Dr. Reaney who ministered in that brokenness in a way I'll never forget.

Our brokenness only undermined the fact of our need for God, and God had sent Dr. Reaney in the nick of time.

Using imagery, he had you exercising an idea that you had used previously, but in a more extensive way. You learned to turn off an invisible button on your arm to close off feeling when a lab tech came by for blood draws.

Dr. Reaney also borrowed your tape entitled "Comfort" and recorded his voice in the foreground—talking to you in his serene manner . . . having you image your bed at home, the feel of your sheets, your curtains, etc. (we had filled him in on information for the descriptions).

It would be a familiar background for you to plug into during scans and tests in the weeks ahead. It would be a piece of home in the unknowns if you imagined it to be so.

By now, even gently hanging your legs from the bed made you irritable. The pressure in your legs and feet was too much. An echocardiogram was scheduled for the next day.

Letting Go

Dear Tommy,

Jesus was always there with you because God came to earth in that way. You and I are linked until we pass through death into His arms. Maybe that is where the "twinkling of an eye" comes from. I miss you –I can't wait to see you again!

Daddy hugged me the other day as that healing issue surfaced again. He was quiet as he listened amidst my tears. Then he said, "Hon, the battle is not in the healing, but in the letting go."

Heart Surgery

Dear Tommy,

As *both* Dr. Marker and Dr. Belani entered your hospital room that noon hour on March 9th, I knew the results of your echocardiogram that morning were bleak. Sure enough, they sat down and shared the news of a mass in the upper left chamber of the heart. As Dr. Marker drew a diagram and went into more detail, I felt like I was having some kind of out-of-body experience—in shock and yet so in control. I had to be.

Dr. Marker asked for Dad's pager number so he could tell him the information and relate the urgency of open heart surgery that afternoon. I had paged Dad a hundred times before, but his number evaded my memory. It did come to mind some minutes later, but all my thoughts had been consumed with, "You're too little to have surgery! We can't be heading for surgery *again*!"

Left alone to ponder the crisis before us, I called Dad and we both cried. I needed him with us more than ever before. Maybe I thought he could sweep it all away... but I knew better—we just needed to *be* together. I sensed that panic in Dad, too—a mutual feeling of being lost.

I hung up and proceeded to relate in detail to you the day's event ahead. For some reason, it all passed right over you. Either I approached you with a barrage of medical jargon to somehow avoid it and try to protect you from my own disbelief and reality, *or* you weren't hearing me.

Because not long before we were headed to the surgery suite, Dad, Dr. Marker, and I sat with you wrapping up last minute details like calling Kristin and Maren and making arrangements for them to be picked up. As you sat in bed, things finally registered and you loudly cried out in exasperation, "You didn't tell me I was going to have *heart surgery*!"

Once again, I went over in simpler language about your heart vegetation and that it was making your hands and feet hurt and would help clear up the sores and take away the pain.

Keeping Vigil

Dear Tommy,

I grin big when I think of what toy you opted to take into heart surgery that time. It was far from the usual fuzzy stuffed animal (several of yours had had their turn). You chose the basketball, given to you by the St. Louis Park girls' team! Their signatures and greetings joyfully covered the ball. Once asleep, I think your heart surgeon was ready to deflate it and get it out of there!

A tall, sturdy-framed man, Dr. Helseth performed the surgery. A highly respected surgeon, it was awesome to me that one so physically grand could operate on the tiniest of babies. *That* in itself was a miracle!

Dad and I held hands as we prayed in a silence of holy trust those next hours. We also nervously ate cookies from the parents' waiting room.

I wanted so badly for you to live. I would rather you die in my arms than alone on a surgery table. My stomach spun as Dad related some details within his own knowledge of heart surgery—that *sometimes* a heart doesn't get pumping again. To think they can stop a heart to operate on it and keep all else alive! Dear God, how could someone *not* believe in you?

Leafing through the little booklet of Bible promises that my godmother Bette had mailed earlier that week, the verse I was drawn to and that became our prayer was:

> My flesh and my heart may fail, but God is the strength of my heart and my portion forever (Ps. 73:26).

I had never seen that verse before, and there it popped out at me during open heart surgery!

My whole soul embraced it and I felt God's peace.

Dad and I also experienced the verse:

The Spirit helps us in our weakness. We do not know what we ought to pray, but the Spirit himself intercedes for us with groans that words cannot express. And he who searches our hearts knows the mind of the Spirit, because the Spirit intercedes for the saints in accordance with God's will (Romans 8:26–27).

I believe there is a point in survival; in keeping vigil, where one's whole being becomes more spiritual than physical.

As a parent of a suffering child, you either suffer with that person or turn away. That's where it must be hard to be a medical caretaker because you *do* interact and are compassionate, and yet you have to be objectively clear, too, to make what are the most responsible and appropriate decisions at that given time. Anyway, in a sense—as much as we were intensely dealing with the physical, the physical had fallen away.

In my vigil with you, Tommy, both our faiths had to kick in full, yes? I see now why I clung so to my faith—to Christ himself—because when it's so pitch-black dark, you can still see with faith. "Because you are my help, I sing in the shadow of your wings. My soul clings to you; your right hand upholds me."

Neither of us was fully consumed in that darkness because Christ is the Light. He says so. And it's true! We walked there—we made it!

In the Company of Angels

Dear Tommy,

What glory! You made it with flying colors, and the Life Support Unit scene repeated itself as we fell into the care once again of your classmate's mom, Kathy. At great ease in her trusted care, we assured you of our presence and eventually went home for the night...scooted out by the staff who knew we needed to tuck a good night's sleep under our belts.

There was often an intense guilt leaving you every night, but even deeper so was a heart-tug that we just wanted you home—need I even mention that the feeling was more than mutual on your part? Each night we had to say good-bye...and good-bye had taken on a whole new meaning with the uncertainty of its finality. Did you know that good-bye is the contraction for "God be with you?"

Quite elated from your post-op state, sleep came easily that night, perhaps because the situation mimicked some sort of aura that *we* were actually in control again. We just may whip this organism after all.

My favorite moment came again that next day as your respirator was removed and your first words were "Apple juice." You even managed to communicate those words with a tube in your mouth the previous hour.

Tommy, I'd go crazy with a respirator. I know you had no choice, but you were a star in my book just for enduring that. You seemed like an old pro at it. The sad thing is that it was true. You were an old pro. As I looked at the line-up of wee ones and older children, I marveled and anguished. It shouldn't be.

And then there was a quadriplegic at your left, Albert. Hit by a car some years back, he was a young boy about your age who always wore a stocking cap. I'm not sure if it was for temperature control or to make a statement of identity—his claim to being him. Anyway, sitting between you two guys could only make me count my blessings. There was no room for pity. Your main concerns were eating and TV viewing—Ninja Turtles and whatever else was of interest.

You and Albert seemed to have some kind of non-verbal bonding. As you witnessed each other's struggles, you seemed to draw encouragement from it and thrived in the reality that you were not alone in your pain. Your stories all dovetailed. All of you kids were drawing strength from an energy that met the Christ within each other.

Even though Albert's limbs didn't move and you would never walk again, there was a spiritual life that was more alive than in the "normal" goings-on. I wonder if that's because you were in the company of angels. You had more time to be still—to allow heaven a space to touch you.

No Greater Love

Dear Tommy,

About this time, Cousin Sharon had come into town. Dad and I popped in to Grandpa and Grandma's that night. We gathered together for food, laughs, and neck rubs. I remember at the table holding back the tears because even though we didn't speak it, we felt the hollow inside that you were absent, Tommy—that perhaps you would never be back. The circle was incomplete without you. But the love was stronger than ever, as was the grief. I began to sense and witness a broader view of what healing really was—sometimes in the body, in the mind, in the spirit, and ultimately in the soul.

I also began to understand that I needed to allow myself to be touched in my hurt. I realized that perhaps there is no greater love than that love received amidst heartache. It was a risk, I'm sure, for people to dare touch our pain. As hard as it was to do, it was the most tender and loving of all touches.

Hit On

Dear Tommy,

A day or two after surgery, one of those off-the-wall happenings took me totally by surprise and bathed me in a wellspring of laughter.

Alone in the hall, this guy about 6 foot 8 comes walking down the hall in a "What's happening?" jiving type of manner. His keys jingled freely from a loop on his jeans as he moved. He stopped me with a comment about my height and declared us a good match. Then, out of the blue, he asked me to lunch! Smiling and a bit flattered, but also terrified inside, I thanked him and told him that I was married. Then, moving out of range, I anxiously looked for Dad.

Funny, huh? It helped lift the whole heart surgery scene into a lighter element. Maybe that was heavenly intent. Could this guy have been an angel?

"What Can I Do?"

Dear Tommy,

"What can I do?" This question echoed over and over about this time. How I wished I had more tangible answers for that. Just love us and pray. The main assistance was with the girls—trying to keep their lives functioning in their world, while yet allowing them to be participants with us and you—their brother, Tommy. The balance is always a challenge with chronic illness and now our focus had shifted. "Life-threatening" was the new theme. So, we tried to be gracious with people's inquiry of "What can I do?" and allowed people to help with food, rides, etc. It was so appreciated! (We began to lean harder, contrary to our nature.)

As we learned once again—people gravitate to drama and generally have an intense momentary response to pitching in. We were set up for a long haul . . . a marathon for which we saw no finish line. We knew it would come, but we became tired and focused and had to be assertive to our needs and desires.

Faith has to hang on and "see" in the thickest of fog and the darkest of darks. Sometimes I think by God's grace, we are even knocked out for a spell and carried in a type of sleep. Hey, that sounds like young parenthood at times!

"You'll be in my prayers" could not be put to action as human promise but sighs fulfilled by heaven.

The Dare

Dear Tommy,

You began to ask questions about how the organism got into your heart and about being born with this disease. As best as I could, I told you, maybe in more detail than you wanted, but you seemed satisfied. I said that this heart surgery should take care of it all. Confident that it would, I felt like my whole foundation of trust with you was shaken as suspicions of a new growth in the *right* atrium of the heart appeared.

Old fears crept back. Should I have taken you in sooner last November instead of December? Would it have made a difference?

I remember when I was nineteen years old, and I took a dare to dive off a dock into one of the coldest lakes in North America, Lake Chelan. This scenario parallels with your hospitalization, Tommy. I felt pushed in. Once I hit the water, my breath was practically nonexistent. There was no turning back. The dock sidings were high and no one else would be able to help me within a safe amount of time. There was only one way—to swim; to swim to shore in any way my body would move. It was a half-block swim in the icy cold. Numb to the bone, I felt very much alive and very happy that I'd made it to shore.

That is a unique type of fight inside that propels one to do what they have to do. It's not because they are necessarily strong or brave. It is because that is the path set before them. And I was glad God was with us.

Anchoring in God's Reality

Dear Tommy,

Later, Dr. Marker helped me see that we were hanging in there well. The perspective that he gave me was commenting that people do survive war zones and concentration camps, etc. I wasn't sure if he meant you, Tommy, or Dad and me. Probably both. I knew this was like an outward-bound experience.

It's similar to a quote by a guy I read about who does Iditasport, the 200-mile race on skis, snowshoes, mountain bikes, or a combo of the three. He said, "You begin to realize how alive you are when you're vulnerable. You begin to understand what survival is all about when you're close to the edge, pushing yourself harder than you've ever pushed before."

God really gave us strength, didn't he, Tommy? Even in our doubts, questions, and not being able to understand so much of what went on, God's love remained constant.

I think about my shock when I went into the music store one day and I no longer found LP records for sale. It was all cassettes, CD's, and videos! I felt left behind; confused. But God doesn't change. If anything, we change to hopefully welcome Him more and more into our lives.

It's like my dear friend Elise told me, "The key is being open about our weaknesses. We need to strengthen our anchor in God's reality because He is creating spaces for something new."

Negotiating with Time

Dear Tommy,

Two days after surgery, I came in at least a half-hour later than I had told you. You greeted me in tears and said, "I was scared. I thought you weren't coming."

Oh, Tommy, if you only knew. Nothing in my power would ever stop me from being with you. My whole world revolved around you.

I told you again that I missed you at home. You said, "I missed you too, Mommy, when *you* were in the hospital." Yeah, that was a time a couple of years back—your maturity and compassion really astounded me. I had to have emergency surgery on a possible appendix problem on Christmas Day 1987. You popped your head out the door as I was leaving: "Mom, do you need me to go with you?" You knew just how it felt, didn't you—to undergo surgery?

These days you reminded me again: "You have someone to cuddle with. I don't."

I became acutely aware that the clock was smack in front of you on a post in the unit. You religiously watched that clock as you monitored your own pain and tolerance or intolerance—and you knew when medicine was due. Sometimes it seemed that you were negotiating with time.

I could just hear your words from a year and-a-half ago at age six . . . fitting for this same setting:

Tommy: "I want to go home."
Mom: "It's been long, hasn't it?"
Tommy: "I can't remember home."

Later you said, "I'm gonna take my operation home."

One time that makes me smile is the day when you guardedly complained about the staff in the life support unit. You said in your high-pitched, sweet whine, "Everyone seems mean here in the LSU."

I said, "It's because they want to help you—sometimes to help you get well, they have to *make* you do certain things."

You seemed content with that answer and relaxed. It seemed to take away a paranoia that these caregivers hated you and picked on you. Ah, what fears and sensitivities are hidden in us all! It's hard to be in tune and anticipate all that they might be. I was glad you could express as you did, Tommy—to reawaken us to a world we were only a part of.

The next MRI and echocardiogram showed no growth on the right atrium, and we were on our way back to 4 East the next day.

Grandma's Stay

Dear Tommy,

March 14. Grandma Doris stayed with you that evening. She writes in her journal: "As I came, Tommy was being given amphotericin. He talked between his teeth asking for pain medicine. I had never really seen the reaction of the 'ampho' before—other than fever. The chills were really intense and he shook considerably. Morphine was administered. By five o'clock, he was interested in a bit of TV, but he complained about his eye. When he sat up, that seemed to help. Perhaps the angle had been bad. We watch together the show about Tony, and I thought he (Tony) was going to be hurt, but Tommy said, 'No, he was just looking him in the eye.'

"An ad about Waikiki reminded me about Hawaii, and then Tommy asked if we had surfed on our recent trip. He fantasized about himself doing it—only lying down and it would be where there are no sharks. When I told him about Grandpa and me catching a twenty-pound tuna, he wondered if I knew how to make tuna fish sandwiches with mayonnaise. That was a golden moment! I said, 'Sure!' He ordered one for tomorrow—with pickles on the side!"

Ongoing Chatter

Dear Tommy,

Before we left the life support unit to move back upstairs, one visit that especially stands out was from my friend, Judy. Glad that she had pushed aside her hesitancy to come, we escaped the physical surroundings of our present reality to the lunchroom.

There in the midst of a friend whose little boy had been born premature and had spent fourteen months in intensive care, the dam broke. I spilled out my fears of death in an ongoing chatter that I knew Judy understood first-hand. Once again, unknowns, unpredictability, and powerlessness loomed over us undisguised. Sure, they are a constant part of all of our lives, but not usually with this intensity . . . with death too close.

Oasis of God's Stillness

Dear Tommy,

Perhaps it was that same day that another special person came into our arena of life and death to stay. It was Bob Flory, the chaplain. He had just returned from a year elsewhere. Leery of my need for a spiritual guide in the previous weeks, I had kept my distance from the woman chaplain who first approached me. Now, the walls inside had begun to melt away, and Bob's presence was simply just that at first—he was present.

I knew he was there and I could request his help. And I also knew that he would keep touching base with our family. In his down-to-earth manner, Bob represented another person in the hospital who stood by us in the role of purely friend—apart from those in the intense circle of caregivers for you, Tommy. In his genuine love, Bob became an oasis of God's stillness and refuge in a world that made less and less sense at times. It is ironic that my own bravery that had imprisoned me, finally evolved into a cry and a thirst for help.

Giving Your Best Shot

Dear Tommy,

Waiting. March 15 was the onset of a ten-day run of continual 103 to 104° fevers. It became another testing time of waiting—of feeling as if our hands were tied, wanting so badly to do something for you.

At 105°, they considered holding back on the white cells and interferon, but I think only the latter was on hold. It was almost like, "Who gives a rip if the interferon is even doing anything?" Getting shots? Yuck!

Sitting up in bed with a patch over your right eye and several scars crossing your chest, you looked war-torn. But the bag of chips you nibbled on on the tray in front of you somehow brought normalcy to the picture. You were still you!

As we began to watch the victorious St. Louis Park girls' basketball game, you perked up. On the wall beside you was the orange poster with the team's photo and caption, "Tommy is our #1 fan." Jill, our friend, occasional baby-sitter, and also co-captain of the team, had given it to you, Tommy, signed by all the team members.

As you watched the tube that night, you commented about Jill, "Oh, that's a good pass!" I reminded you that they had dedicated the last game to you. You then said, "Maybe they're trying to win this game for me, too. But even if they don't win, they are really good!"

And so, paralleled by thoughts about you, Tommy, in this world we knew your body may not "win" in the way we would like; but we knew that you already had won in Jesus Christ. He takes the pressure off because the victory is ultimately His!

That night as you rallied between your own discomfort and the TV, you were asleep long before Jill's team won. Even in your sleep, you were battling—no doubt playing your own game... and I know, too, giving your best shot.

The Chasm

Dear Tommy,

As I think back, I remember that night before watching the basketball game, we saw the half-hour show "Why, Charlie Brown, Why?" (a story by Charles M. Schulz about what happens when a friend is very ill).

Rarely insistent on much, I encouraged you to watch it—almost to the point of my own desperation for you to see it. I can't even remember if the girls were with us in your room that evening, but you were obviously glued to the set. I needed so badly for you to be face-to-face with an objective situation you could identify with. I needed to begin talking with you more frankly about death—about your own death. Who was I to say—or to know—if you would live through this, or when you would die?

It was a neat show and allowed for some soul-searching and feelings and questions. But Janice, the girl who struggled with leukemia in the story, did get better and returned to school. I worried that you would internalize failure if *you* didn't get well.

There was such a silence between you and me at the end of that program, Tommy. It was a chasm of some of the deepest of feelings... perhaps where both our pain and our love blended as one—a glimpse of God's pain for us, His hope, and His peace that passes all understanding.

Two Little Tablets

Dear Tommy,

The heart surgery seemed to dissolve your pain. The fungi in the heart had been where the blood could carry it out everywhere—kind of like your heart was a showerhead and the water spraying out was all the vessels poisoning your entire system. That's why your feet and hands hurt so much and you manifested a rash. The fungi began to seed and grow. Fungi are so nasty. This one was especially relentless.

The completion and supposed success of heart surgery brought a high to our emotions. All seemed wrapped up in a final packaged answer... but not for long.

The high fevers triggered questions of a new mass. Was it in the heart again? I wondered even about AIDS and if somehow you had been the "luck of the draw" and picked up mono, CMV, or AIDS in these blood transfusions you got routinely. Dr. Marker sensed the concern in me regarding AIDS and had you tested for it. He said that was something we didn't need to have hanging over our heads—we already had plenty to worry about.

An echocardiogram was to be scheduled for the first of the week. I remember feeling like you were dead in my arms as the Tylenol wore off. But as soon as you got your Tylenol, you were a different kid. You would have been quite a plus in a TV commercial for that drug company. I truly felt like those little tablets raised you from the dead! For these seemingly small gifts, we were so grateful! In *our* book, they were big miracles in themselves.

Invisible Faith

Dear Tommy,

About this time, I was glad we had gone to see *The Ten Commandments* at the movie theater the summer before. You and the girls sat through those four hours aided by popcorn and candy and *of course* a brief intermission to hit the toilet. But those things that are God-centered and that which is good and pure to think on are worth it. As what I dreaded would be—that your life here was perhaps ending sooner than we thought—one reflects on the meat of where you've been in this life, how you have lived, and what love you have given. The perspective of asking oneself in all situations, "Now, what would Jesus do?" is idealistic being human, but one to strive for, because His strength does give us that power to follow Christ. What really matters becomes clearer in that hour when death shoves its face nose-to-nose with your own.

I acutely felt the first visible step was happening as you had vision in only one eye left, Tommy. Oh, man, did that ever get to us.

All together, one night we decided to see the movie, *Mary and Joseph* on video in your hospital room. Maren was in protest at first. She had another choice. But, as we watched, it was obvious that this was a good one for us all to see at the same time.

In essence, the movie was about Mary and Joseph integrating their walk with God into their own lives amidst many life trials that tested their faith . . . and deeply questioned it.

Once again, it struck me how this young woman, Mary, believed that she was pregnant with the Son of God and yet she couldn't feel Him at first and couldn't see Him. Somehow though, she knew for sure. She believed.

That same faith was what we had to draw on. You were not healed bodily in the earthly sense, Tommy. Some say there is a faith that does that...a miracle of healing that one can see. This type of faith, we had to ride with in another way...that opened us to resting in God's will and knowing and believing that His kind hand and His love was upon you—as He had told me it would be in that dream before you were born.

It's not exactly easy to be beaten up and still believe.

Gaining Entry

Dear Tommy,

Dr. Reaney sent home a videotape called "No Fears, No Tears." If I recall correctly, it was about children coping with illness from the emotional angle to dealing with needles.

Perhaps he gave me the video to help you deal more calmly with needle pokes and for me to be a proper encouraging support. But, the movie's title evoked the opposite. It became an outlet for me to let out my own tears and fears. In a sense, the cleansing had given me permission to release some of my pain. In my own survival walls I had around me, Dr. Reaney had creatively gained entry to my darkness.

The Regret

Dear Tommy,

I especially regret one thing, and that was not having implemented more "safe times" for you—certain hours of the day where no lab person, no respiratory therapist, doctor, or nurse could invade your space. I am so sorry. Your interruptions were endless. But, we did get home now and then. Even though you were off IV fluids during those hours, the drought was worth it, eh? Nothing can fill the soul like a visit home, can it?

Spiritual Getaway

Dear Tommy,

About this time, Dr. Marker wanted you to be on IV fluids round-the-clock at the hospital, so home passes took a halt. I think you hardly noticed with your fever spikes.

Ha! Remember that day I was so blasted tired? (Which one, huh?) Anyway, you had coaxed me to stay overnight and I agreed. As it got later, I felt unusually restless and knew this was not a good evening to stay. In an attempt to break our friendly verbal contract, I was desperate enough to offer you five bucks if I could wait a night. You looked at me so sweetly and said, "Mom, you're worth more than five dollars!"

You so wanted me to stay. But it was one of those once in a while times when one needs out, and I weaseled my way out of the deal. It was another move on my part that was so validated, and yet heaped the guilt on for weeks after.

You must have known that was an important night because the following night as I lay next to you twenty-four hours later, you were much sicker and vomiting much of the night. You had told Grandma the next day, "My mom can lie down without throwing up, but I can't."

That night made me aware once again that your world was constant. You couldn't really leave and take a break—even if it felt like the walls were swallowing you up. Your getaway had to be spiritually . . . an inner dependency on Jesus.

You talked to Grandma about fishing on the dock at a place that we had visited last summer with hopes of doing it again. Catching "sunnies" was a treat, and you envisioned boating with Dad.

"I'm not feeling good." That phrase of yours echoed in real life and in our heads. I so wished we could trade places for a while, at least. You always agreed on that one!

Coping Tools

Dear Tommy,

Grandma told me that you had inquired about Grandpa. "Grandpa gave blood, didn't he?" You and Grandma talked about all the people who had donated blood on your behalf. You told her that you'd never give it. Gee, I wonder why, pal?

Then I heard about the respiratory therapist who came in and said, "I would like to get to know you, Tommy. Your grandma tells me you like fishing? I've fished a lot in northern Minnesota..." You responded, "Let's not do any talking now."

I wondered how that woman took your comment. It made me feel deeper than ever that you, Mr. Social Guy, were on an inward-bound experience, so focused and delving into any kind of equipment you had inside to hang on. In contrast to the rest of us, your world was life and death—you had to go it alone to a degree.

Dr. Cohen, a more outspoken, hang-loose personality—and not as visibly traditionally dressed as Dr. Reaney—talked with me one day while Dr. Reaney was gone. He, too, dealt with pain. He gave me his tips on helping you facilitate your anger and discomfort with nausea and all.

Incorporating his ideas into my time with you, I suggested you figure out a color for your anger, let it slip down your arm, tighten your fist, hold it, and toss it. Then you were supposed to tell me what color it was. I'm not sure how much it helped you, but sometimes I think some of these tools are secretly for the parents; like when you buy a new toy for your kid and you end up enjoying it more than they do!

Another idea was to lick your finger and put it on your forehead. Lastly, I told you to imagine a cool popsicle and the wind. You said in a tired, fed-up manner, "Mom, it would be easier to imagine if you'd just blow on me." I still laugh at that one.

His Ways

Dear Tommy,

March 19th—three months in the hospital already!

I remember going home one morning to escape. Grandma was there doing laundry, and I unloaded the recent medical tidbits. Dr. Marker didn't seem too "up" with the echocardiogram results. There was a shadow that had elongated. Dr. Belani examined your hurting knees with only an answer really of "No fluid." I couldn't read her mind, and I ached to know more. So did she. And the eye doctor who examined your eye did not like the looks of the redness—something was fighting. And your teacher called again, Tommy, to encourage us and also to remind us not to give up. I think the combination of the various diagnoses and messages at times wore one to the core. The vigil and grind is almost indescribable to one who has not walked there.

Before you were born, Tommy, the world of medicine and faith seemed filled with answers that were more clear-cut. No longer true, I did want to give up sometimes; I did want answers *now*! But, this world wasn't loaded with Band-Aids for quick fixes. It was loaded with land mines, floods, valleys, mountaintops, sunshine and rain, lightning and summer breezes. I learned that the world was really a mission field to draw people back to the God who made them. It is as simple as that. His ways—as much as we longed to know—were not ours for this time to know.

Doctor's Wife

Dear Tommy,

I wasn't always so sure if being a doctor's wife was an asset and yet, in some ways, I think it was.

My personality wasn't demanding to begin with, but I feared that if I was too assertive, someone would interpret that as me saying I deserved better treatment and more attention because I'm a doctor's wife. And I didn't need any more conflict. Those things can be more of a blown-up fear than anything—and it really isn't fair to others to even entertain those thoughts. In so many ways, my hypersensitivity was under fire, and I continued to pray for some outer crust and endurance. When I was a child, my parents said I took things to heart almost too much and was unusually sensitive. In one vein, I wondered if that was so true, why did God give you to me? And yet, as a part of me crumbled inside, He rebuilt a new piece of me that included Him through and through—sort of like how character building must happen.

So often I wondered about Dad's thoughts. As a physician, he has tossed and turned and wrestled with certain patients of his who were about to die or in a crisis. I knew that our doctors had the same mind-set. As controlled as they seemed on the outside, their "innards" told a different story.

The Smile

Dear Tommy,

Your heart status remained the same, or got better. They would continue to keep an eye on the right atrium. Dr. Marker has been in favor of surgery, but heart surgeon, Dr. Helseth, says no.

There was always great rejoicing when you'd eat—two whole tacos despite that ongoing 104° temperature. See, Tylenol gets the edge again!

It was that day when a rare golden moment took place. I was thrilled to have witnessed it. As I lay alongside you under your blanket from home, I started gently teasing you. You did likewise. Suddenly, like the sun peeking through a cloudy sky, your precious smile appeared, followed by a laugh. I could write a psalm about that!

When I tasted that moment, I realized then how dark things really had been. So, this is what hope must be. In two minutes, my spirit was refueled for the long month that lay ahead.

God's Extended Arm

Dear Tommy,

Ringing in one ear became a new concern—possibly a drug side effect.

So many unknowns. White cells, interferon, very high doses of amphotericin, five antibiotics, eye medications, morphine, Valium, and something for the stomach. Seems they would interrupt each other or cancel out the effectiveness of each other. Once again, seven years old seemed too young and small to handle it all.

Dr. Marker sat and talked to me one evening in your room after your daily check-in exam on rounds. He seemed to be grappling himself with all that was going on—trying to help make sense of it for me.

Knowing Dr. Marker would be leaving for vacation in two days, I prayed that if you were going to die, Tommy, that he would be in town. His being your primary doctor, I had latched onto him. He had slowly become Christ's extended arm—my in-person visible model for the Great Physician in heaven. Dr. Marker was one person who could get away with saying, "I understand." Somehow whether he really did or didn't, I believed him. In his soft-spoken way, he reassured Dad and me that the girls would be okay in all of this. He had the ability to quietly cut through the crap and zero in on the parent. Perhaps it is because he was only too well acquainted with the arena of chronic illness and infectious diseases. My sense is that he had an unusual insight on human nature.

That gave him an edge with being sensitive to parents. My guess is as intense as it is working with long-term sick kids, there is more of a tolerance on both the physician's and parent's parts in treatment. The element of humor is there as well. Without it, there was no salt of the earth, so to speak.

A Greater Power

Dear Tommy,

From a young age, your sense of your length of years seemed pronounced. You knew your body played havoc with you at times, but you also made every good moment count.

Once at age four, you hugged me and said, "Let's talk about dying. I don't want you to die."

Later that year, I told you, "God's power is not in swords or guns like He-Man. There's a greater power."

You said, "We don't have any."

I said, "If we have God, we do. Then we have a *power in our heart.*"

We talked about how we are a part of God's Son. You concluded, "God is my weapon!"

You had that power in your heart. One day after Dad and I had returned from a trip, you kids and I were at a shopping mall. Walking by a wishing well, you tossed in a nickel and came back to me with outstretched arms, "I wished that I could hug you."

Might this be the simple invitation to all from Jesus? Come!

You obviously said "yes" to God each day and were well equipped with the greatest of these—love!

The Question

Dear Tommy,

Whether it was intuition, the Holy Spirit, or coincidence (actually, they do dovetail), the timing on my visits to the chaplain and social worker was perfect.

First, I made an appointment with Jerome, the social worker, and spilled out my fears about death, the "what ifs," and my need to extend my thoughts to the unfamiliar territory of funeral arrangements. Jerome reassured me of the latter—if that time came, people would come to my aid and pitch in. That put my mind so at ease because as much as I pushed the thought of death away, I also had to confront reality. And I needed to know some facts so that I could set certain wondering and worry aside and be the friend, mom, and caregiver I wanted to be to the utmost.

Next, I sought out counsel with Bob, the chaplain who also had befriended us. I had a deep need to just talk and rattle off my nervous energy and fears once again. Between the two of these guys, I was able to verbalize with them my all-thumbs feeling about directly asking you, Tommy, about dying. Bob gave me some solid possibility on how to word the question that ached inside. It needed to come out but was choked within a paralyzing terror that if I asked you . . . I was certain your death sentence would be confirmed.

So, on March 22, 1990, I sat at the end of your bed with Dad in a chair beside you. Somewhere in our conversation, it felt like the feelings blurted out. "It must be hard being sick so much." You said, "Yes, I feel terrible." Then, I think only by the grace of God, I was able to quite calmly ask, "Do you feel like you're dying?"

Sounding a tinge perturbed by the question, you said, "No." I wasn't sure if you were offended or what by the question, but I didn't care. I had asked it. And we knew that you were full of fight. It gave us new wind to stand that ground of helping you in any way we could—of hoping with you, of loving you without a looming fear in our midst. It was full speed ahead.

Impending Absence

Dear Tommy,

One last time before his family vacation, Dr. Marker checked on you. All his patients connected him with peanut M&M's—he always had a supply on hand in his clinic. I remember you'd go away from an appointment with full pockets!

The setting was the hospital scene that Friday night. A whole week lay ahead with Dr. Marker's impending absence, and I feared that you might not make it, Tommy. I was afraid that because Dr. Marker was leaving, that everything would go on hold. Once again, I so wanted to know, "Is Tommy going to die?" The nagging question lay buried inside.

I felt sorry for this man and his family, who on the verge of vacation, were supposed to kick back and enjoy life. I wondered how he compartmentalized his very, very sick patients and redirected that time to his family. It must have torn at him to leave. But he did have another life.

I sure didn't want Dr. Marker to go. As a parent of a patient, I think on one hand I was angry that he did go. I felt abandoned. On the other hand, my heart went out to his wife—a woman I know I could easily identify with, being a doctor's wife myself. And here I was on the other side now again with a sick child, being a part of that constant demanding pull that the hospital is for physicians and their families. Things just don't wrap up neatly each weekend.

As Dr. Marker left that night after a brief exam and chat, I wanted to at least tell him that we would miss him, but words just didn't come. There had been some comfort in his presence. Now it was gone. Who knew where we would all be in seven days upon his return?

The Host

Dear Tommy,

Your classmate buddy, Chris, stopped by that night with his dad and siblings, while his mom was working in LSU.

You played it real cool as they gathered to ask how you were. Clad in your blue hospital PJ bottoms, you leaned back in your pillow with your arms under the back of your head and said, "Hmmm . . . I'm okay." I remember the tears welling up in Chris's dad's eyes. His ability to display his compassion in that way was one that I envied in people and also a gift that gave me a wonderful warmth of communication that words needn't accompany. I found out later that his dad had died when he was a child. That, along with severe back problems, perhaps had connected him to both of us, Tommy, in his own pain.

After they left, your staged performance quickly dissolved and you were swallowed up in your discomfort once again.

It was a late night by the time I left. Sometimes Dad would come later and stay on so I could get to the girls before bedtime. They had their share of mealtimes with us on trays in your room, too.

Itraconazole was increased to two, every eight hours. You were a master at pill swallowing—ones the size that even adults could choke on!

All-Alert

Dear Tommy,

March 24. The date is forever etched in my mind.

A Saturday morning...ahhh...it felt good to get a little sleep.

The moment I called in and talked to your nurse, my adrenaline went into high gear. Briefing me about the night happenings, my all-alert system hit a panic state. As Ann told me of headaches and blurred vision, I knew then that they mustn't wait for the CT scan scheduled for Monday. My urgency was far from hidden, and I couldn't seem to get to the hospital fast enough. I told Ann that you needed the scan as soon as possible. They had to take action.

It was obvious to me, Tommy, that your condition had changed radically and my Swedish reserve left me. In tears, I was grateful for a nurse who had gotten on the stick and told Dr. Belani the situation. They were wise to listen to a parent's mind that day—I salute them! As I was to hear my own heart...or I would have regretted it the rest of my days. Assured that you were heading to the CT scan that morning, my relief came flooding out.

Weak with intense headaches, your right side and cheek were puffy.

As we left 4 East that day, I had a guarded hope that we would return. It was too hard to say good-bye. I probably smiled—maybe even tried to joke around to ease the tension in the air.

These nurses on this unit had become my family. It wasn't fair. Any of it.

The Bleed

Dear Tommy,

As you endured another CT scan, I knelt down next to you with my x-ray protector smock and held your hand. No doubt we had your tape player going above the hum of the scanner with x-ray technician, Bruce, not far away.

I opened the little booklet that Bob, the chaplain, had given me the other day. Entitled "Water Bugs and Dragonflies," it was a beautiful story to help explain death to children. As happened once again, it was, to me, the story that spoke.

Things moved quickly now. Wheeled out into the hall, I could see a neurologist and several radiologists convening over x-rays. The doctors came out to deliver the news. It appeared to be that there was some internal bleeding in your brain. You would need to go into surgery as soon as possible.

All I could do was agree—whatever you say, Doc! And as for you, I think you had drifted elsewhere, Buddy, and your headaches became more intense. I told you that they were going to take care of your headaches and do some surgery. I began to feel my tears well up. I wanted Dad to hurry and get there.

Parked in a corner bed of the life support unit, a curtain was drawn to the side of us. As I tended to you, Tommy, to try to get you settled, two arms encircled me from behind. Such a familiar comforting squeeze. It was Daddy. He had made it! Relieved, I sobbed.

We were momentarily hustled off together by the neurosurgeon who was on call that weekend. He brought us to a room where he succinctly pointed out what he thought was the problem, and what he would do . . . drain the "bleed" and check the head and sinuses. I'll never forget him saying, "God willing, that will take care of it."

Not Forgotten

Dear Tommy,

I trusted these surgeons through and through, or did I? What other choice did we have?

You wanted water so badly, but surgery was imminent, and that was a no-no. As we wheeled you past other beds toward the operating room, my eyes caught the eyes of two nurses that you had had in LSU. The tears were not to be contained.

The compassionate glance of these nurses spoke so deeply of their concern and love for you and for us all. We definitely were not alone in this.

A strange silence consumed us. Brain surgery: the surgeon had made it sound simple enough. Might this resolve the ten days of high fever? You hadn't walked in two and a half weeks. At least something was happening; something concrete was being done. We called Grandma to bring the girls to the hospital.

It was in the unknown and emptiness that Dad and I routinely searched out some sort of tranquillity in the chapel.

As we entered, the place was totally dark for the first time. Some light had always been lit in a sort of peaceful welcome. Did this darkness symbolize what was to come?

I remember praying with heart and soul, telling God if your mind wasn't left, to please take you. I knew you wouldn't have wanted to live the life of a vegetable, and I wanted to at least voice my opinion.

On the wall of the chapel, the name "Tom" was etched into the wall quite obscurely near the back pew. I always sat in the back right corner, but it was the first time I noticed it. The name reminded me of you being carved on the palms of His hands—a verse that became a favorite:

I will not forget you! See, I have engraved you on the palms of my hands (Isaiah 49:15).

No, He would not forget you, Tommy!

The Miraculous Nightmare

Dear Tommy,

Grandpa, Grandma, Kristin, and Maren were there in the waiting room as your surgery began. Dad explained to us all how three holes would be drilled on the right side of your skull and a semi-circular flap would be cut to expose the area.

Time passed and everyone went home, except Dad and me. It was a late afternoon on a Saturday, so we were quite alone.

Unable to fathom that our son was being operated on in this fashion, our minds methodically turned to food. Even though hunger was not an issue, we knew we had to eat. Midway through the food line, a nurse interrupted us to get back upstairs. We kind of wondered because we had seen your doctor in the stairwell in surgery garb. His demeanor looked extremely preoccupied and frantic.

Soon enough we knew why. What transpired in the following hours was nothing short of a miracle.

In the operating room, Dr. Nagib spotted an aneurysm as he drained blood from your brain (if there hadn't been blood, the aneurysm wouldn't have shown up or have been found). In order to see which vessel to clamp, they needed a good picture. So you headed through the tunnel to Abbott Hospital for an angiogram (part of your skull was left at Children's Hospital and the flap was loosely closed temporarily—gross, huh?). As you were on the table about to get an angiogram, someone screamed as the aneurysm burst. Without a picture, you were hastily moved back through the long tunnel to the Children's Hospital operating room. The loose flap on your skull allowed the flow of blood externally. If it had been sealed, you no doubt would have died.

Remarkably so, blood pressure remained stable and strong. They inserted a line into the groin to give blood, along with your port-a-cath and two other sights of entry—I believe in your arms.

The phone call in the waiting room left us in depressed spirits. Hearing that the aneurysm had burst and that you were in the process of being stabilized, we knew this could be it. This could be the end.

The next step of finding the vessel and clamping it was tedious, intricate, and I'm sure at least doubly complicated without a picture to guide Dr. Nagib.

Meanwhile, Kathy and Chris came by. I was mixed up as to whether we needed to be alone or with other people. Despite the fact that we barely knew these people, we had been quickly bonded in the last weeks through crisis. We all hugged each other. I remember sobbing on Kathy's shoulder and worrying that I'd ruin her leather coat with my salty tears.

We talked a while, trying to prepare ourselves for the news that we would be going home with an empty blanket that night.

The phone rang again. I didn't want to pick it up. I needed to hold hope as long as I could.

Dad answered. In an incredibly short amount of time—about one hour—Dr. Nagib had gone into a deep area that fed the aneurysm and clamped it.

Such high drama it was!

Kathy's and Chris's presence had linked our low and our high that night. They left, and we eagerly awaited the chance to see you, our son.

Dr. Nagib came out and expressed the ordeal as a "nightmare." He looked worn. I think he was also in a state of shocked elation. I gave him a big, happy hug. Later, Dave, who did anesthesia, got a hug, too. Dave said, "In one year, we'll look back and talk about what a miracle this was!"

Whether you lived fifty more years or only one more week, we were in seventh heaven.

The Guarded High

Dear Tommy,

I was in awe of the hell that could break loose with the genetic set-up I'd passed on to you, my son, in combo with a rampant organism. One lousy X chromosome changed the response of your white cells to certain bacteria and fungi. How intricately we are made!

Back to the brain surgery—it had taken one and-a-half hours to close up your skull and flesh. I don't let my mind sit long in thought about it. As grateful and thrilled as I was with the outcome, the details I held at a distance.

The next hours would tell us much... whether you could still talk, think, make sense... whatever! On a super guarded high, I would not sleep until I heard.

An unexpected call from our first home place on 4 East invited us upstairs. There before us in the conference room, a double bed had been put together on the floor with mattresses and sheets. On the table to our right sat a pitcher of water and napkins. That deed spoke loudly of a love that we also felt towards them all. It was a community experience that I hadn't been such an intense part of since my year in the mountains at Holden Village sixteen years ago. It was a genuine replica of what life must have been like when Christ walked among His followers and spread His Father's love with endless parables and stories.

My mind wandered often to the people who also cared for you, Tommy. I knew we were your family, but all these people here couldn't help but become an extended family in a sense. I'm sure their job at the hospital had to be in constant check with certain boundaries. Those may have included issues of touch, emotions, and other invested interests with patients and families that time and human limitations had to resist temptation to become involved. To straddle between dealing with one's natural draw of love in one's heart versus the horrid nature of job burnout, I'm sure was not easy for the staff.

Dad and I washed up in the shower and trundled off to bed in a daze. With a job that demanded adequate sleep, Dad dozed off quickly. I lay wide awake. I had never felt so alive . . . so suspended in time . . . so animated.

As my heart and head replayed the miracle over and over again, I felt ecstatically jubilant and didn't see how God would take you now that He saved you—and in such a dramatic way. I prayed once again for your mind to be intact.

They had spoken of your unusually stable blood pressure throughout the ordeal with such joy and pride. It was as if you had graduated with some kind of honors. You had hung in there with a fighting determined spirit. I knew you were still giving your all with God at your side.

Midnight. One A.M. Two A.M. If those in the recovery room had known I was awake, I'm sure they would have called us first. But, with great hesitation, I dialed downstairs. And why not? You were my son!

Then, in the minutes that followed, the staff relayed the glorious news. You were doing well. As they said, "Tommy is responding appropriately." I felt our spirits touch in a glow of a reunited kinship. You were back! You were still with us in the way that I had so longed for.

Unable to settle down, my eyes must have fluttered and fought a much-needed sleep for the next four hours. Maybe my wakefulness was like a holy night—long watch. I could taste life in its rawness. In the post-surgery danger of the next days, time was sacred. I had to remain alert.

And maybe, too, it was simply that I was a mother!

Grandma's Journal

Reflecting on last night with the girls, there were some tender moments. At different times, I did hold each in my lap and rocked Kristin. Maren had fixed what she wanted for supper, but the news of the aneurysm had rocked us all. She cried, "Tommy could die. What if that happens? I'm not sure where heaven is." She wouldn't eat supper but sat on my lap and we talked about life and death, Jesus, heaven, etc., both of us crying in between.

The phone rang, and it was Jane with the words: "A small miracle" but it really turned out to be a big one—finding the blood vessel to clamp and finishing the surgery. I could tell Maren that even as we were crying out, God heard us and answered...Kristin seemed shook up by all of this, but was quieter. It was good to hold her later and talk a bit...I slept intermittently with my head abuzz and Tommy always there.

An Invitation to Love

Dear Tommy,

So eager for morning to come, Dad and I left our hospital honeymoon suite and headed to witness life in you. In shock and floating on a new spiritual plane, we looked as if we had been at an all-night party. But, we were oblivious to it all, except you.

Stretched out once again on an LSU bed under those bright lights, you had white bandages around your head, turban style, and tubes— it seemed everywhere. Your right eye was blackening. Your body was swollen, and there was that nose tube and respirator again.

To most anyone else, I'm sure you looked like a pretty horrible-looking tough cookie, but to us you were a wonderful sight to behold. You were beautiful! You were alive!

One never was sure where to touch you or what felt good, but there were your hands. You loved to have your hand held. I'll never forget that squeeze of response you gave me that day. It was an invitation to love.

And also, I remember how you dug your nails in my palm to signal pain and that I must do something about it.

I remember thinking many times that the crucifixion couldn't have been much worse. I knew it must have been, though—and no morphine! Jesus Christ must have felt horribly alone.

He was ridiculed and scoffed.

He was beaten up verbally and bodily.

His spirit must have died in God's arms that day He died on the cross.

It must have been in that acknowledgment of death that the Father, Son, and Holy Spirit truly became One—united to save His people.

Death will happen for each one of us. That reality He

does not deny, but in one's death in the belief of Jesus Christ, a hope is real... there is a door out.

In a world that delights in and almost worships fantasy, here is a God in whom all can partake if they choose. He is like our vision of a world of magic and fantasy, except it extends beyond that, it is *for real.*

Nonverbal Dialogue

Dear Tommy,

Our communication exchange had to be on a restricted 'yes' or 'no' basis. You could nod your head, and we figured things out from there. It's amazing how much "dialogue" actually took place in that manner. I'm sure there were times when you'd like to have told us to shut up, too—in your words, it would have been "Be quiet!"

Dad and I could sit for hours next to you and marvel at what mankind could do with God's resources. You were alive! If you hadn't responded to us—if your brain had been obviously altered or impaired, I think those feelings would have been totally different, edged with an overwhelming sorrow.

I remember Grandma telling us about when she and Grandpa relieved us at the hospital for a spell. They told you, "We'll be with you for a while until Mom and Dad return, okay?" You nodded your head. You became a bit restless and the nurse inquired about your pain. You nodded again. Morphine was administered. It was so good to hear of you reacting and responding! Then, while Grandpa was turning over the tape on your little red player, Grandma said she started humming softly. Immediately in protest, you *shook* your head! To my little guy who savored silence and knew what he wanted, it was a bit of humor for the grandfolks in the midst of your situation.

Cranial pressure, blood pressure, heart rate, etc.—all were being monitored. Two drugs that were new for you were Dilantin, given to prevent seizures, and Decadron, to reduce swelling.

In the hype of it all, there was perhaps too much commotion for your post-op state, but family did trickle in. At one point, Pastor Groehler laid hands on you in anointing, prayer, and Scripture, as Kristin and Maren, Dad and I, Grandpa and Grandma, and your godmother/cousin Michelle, gathered around. It was a very centered moment in thanks. Though practically motionless, you were the hub of so many thoughts and prayers around the world. In that way, you were a connector of hearts. It was also a comfort to us all—one that in itself was the assurance that we conveyed to you time and again: "So many people love you, Tommy, and are praying for you."

As onlookers, it looked as if you were being tortured. It was bad stuff. But in the quiet, I heard God's voice telling me what to pass on to you. I said, "God loves you, Tommy. You're *so* special! He told me His hand is on you and to be at peace."

God had reminded me once again of this message from those dreams before you were born. When worldly sense had no foundation, God gave me His refuge.

Stay Close

Dear Tommy,

Spanning an interval of seventy years, the godparents we'd chosen for you almost eight years before were 13-year-old cousin, Michelle, and 83 year-old great-grandpa, Elmer. You no doubt would beat both to the grave.

Memories clicked back some years when Grandpa Elmer's wife, Grandma Elvina, died of Alzheimer's disease. Grandpa Elmer seemed a bit baffled by people coming up to him after she died, saying it was good she was released from her struggles here. But, no—Grandpa just wanted her around still... her presence had been a comfort despite the long bus ride to the nursing home.

Ya know, Tommy, that's how I felt. In one way, I thought: "Enough of this suffering!" On the other hand, it was everything just to be able to touch your warm skin and know you were alive and present.

In the weeks to come, I would be thrilled just to hold you, sometimes waiting all day just to rock you for a few minutes.

Two other people who came by were Uncle Paul and Aunt Bernice. After Paul saw you, he reflected on his experience in Iwo Jima and wondered how you could endure such a battle there at the hospital. It was a reality that I think horrified him. He thought some of that imagery stuff might have come in handy in those foxholes during wartime.

That night, Dad and I braved another sleepover at the hospital, but this one was spent in a tiny conference room—enough air for the seven hours. Your crisis wasn't yet over and we needed to be near. We needed to be able to tell you that we were close, too.

The Sweetest Joy

Dear Tommy,

The words of your neurosurgeon and anesthesiologist continued to ring in my head with a reckless sort of gaiety.

"There's no way anyone survives this (referring to the recent aneurysm episode), being a third of a mile away from the operating room and having it burst. Something happened! Medically, you don't have a 'save' like this. Just the timing of everything . . . quite miraculous."

But on March 26 when your respirator was taken out, the word that held the sweetest joy of all came from your lips, Tommy. As you sat up and laid your head gingerly against me, you said, "MOMMY."

The cranial pressure tube would come out the next day, and it felt like we were all growing wings.

You looked *so* good! But pain lurked constantly, and even though I wasn't walking your experience with physical hurting, medical apparatus and all, I tried to at least be sensitive to your side of it. But the truth is, at that point we were on a high. You felt crummy, though, didn't you?

So, we longed to comfort you.

That evening, a big surprise awaited us. A Chinese dinner was bagged up for us with a note: *"You're always 'Primary' with us! Enjoy. We love you!"*

Ann, Kelly, Heidi, Laurie, and Faith. Such warmth and caring—and it was a practical way , too, to touch our pain. It helped to know that 4 East, our floor for most of the last three months, hadn't disconnected from us. It was a real joy when they'd briefly pop by just to say hi.

At times the attention I know aggravated you and that only made sense—you felt lousy and were seriously ill. We were out on a unit with beds separated only by a curtain with lights on round-the-clock. I'd have gone loony in there as a patient!

Another World

Dear Tommy,

This period of time was reminiscent of the time when Dad and I were lost on a backpack trip in the Sierra Mountains. Our permit allowed us to choose to depart from the path and go cross-country into some quite deserted lakes.

After two nights at various spots of incredible beauty where the sky was bluer than blue and the lake fresh and crystal clear, we proceeded to catch the trail beyond a high pass and over some rocky terrain.

For seven hours we hiked over boulders in the hot sun—a seemingly endless pursuit. I felt trapped with boulders stretching as far as I could see all around me. The only answer was to press onward in the direction that we had committed our steps to.

As dusk lay several hours ahead, we stopped, put our packs down and proceeded to inch toward a promising spot. But, as we got there, the scene below took my breath away. On an overhang, we witnessed an eagle soar below us, and beneath the bird lay a frozen lake. How high had we come? Where were we? Would we ever get back to the earth again? What happened?

Eventually, we wandered to a meadow skirted in dense forest. Below the meadow lay a stretch of flat rock and waterfall.

In that lostness I felt terrified. Dad had a good sense of where we were by then, but I didn't trust him. I found no comfort in him. He tried to explain it with the map, but my fear blocked my grasp of his knowing. So like us and God, eh?

Along with my tears, darkness fell and I had to let go.

After a restless sleep, we hiked several miles to where a human path joined our world. I so wanted to hug the first person whom I saw. I wanted to scream, "Oh, it's wonderful to see you! If you only knew where we've been!"

Blind

Dear Tommy,

Perhaps it was about March 27th. "He doesn't see." As I spoke those words, the impact of that reality seared into my being... into places I didn't even know I could feel.

The helplessness we felt was horrible as we watched you try to figure out how to lie down. You had no understanding at the moment of spatial orientation.

Dr. Ramsay was calling all over the country for possible solutions. One eye's sight was gone—but the other had a chance to regain vision. But the eye mass was worsening. You were blind.

Ponderings

Dear Tommy,

    I remember sitting alone with you in the life support unit—beds to our left and right. You were sitting up in a dreamy sort of stupor, and quietly in your sweet way of reflection said, "I wish it was two years before." My head and heart scrambled to think of a way to take away this pain and fix it, but I could only listen with a reply, "Oh, Tommy, you mean like when you were running and playing and really healthy?" You said, "Yes" with a subtle nod.

    What burdens for one so young to shoulder!

    We learned that you had lost about five times what your blood volume had been. That was one cue to request more blood donations from church and friends.

    Holding you always drew an ecstatic response from me. It felt good to see your head bandage come off and wash all the blood out of your hair. Then we read a book that a former babysitter, Dana, sent you. You were actually intent on listening . . . even so much as to hear it twice!

The Advocates

Dear Tommy,

Anxiety rode high that day as your pain and medication were at odds. I wanted to make my own PCA (Pain Control Anesthesia) pump and fix your hurt. It was a yucky run of hours as the anesthetist explained your situation and how finding the balance, amount, and type of meds for each patient varies. Brain surgery had its own aftermath agenda. As far as I was concerned, you had no time to quibble with that.

Both Nurse Tami and I hit the ceiling and pleaded as patient advocates for help. Eventually, things got under control.

Dave would have liked to have put your nurse and me on eight milligrams of some sedative while you got four. It was an awful time not to be able to protect you.

The Brief Visit

Dear Tommy,

    As the heart surgeon, Dr. Helseth, roamed by your bed one evening, I eye-balled him and told him outright that I was glad he was stubborn. He had refused to do a second heart surgery at that time. If he had done a second surgery to remove the new vegetation, you no doubt would have been dead because the aneurysm (unbeknownst to us at the time) would have burst into a closed skull on the operating table. First things first! I couldn't imagine you being in shape for any more surgery.

    Dr. Helseth smiled in acknowledgment. As he spoke, his words reflected great puzzlement as to why you stood in such a predicament, Tommy. He wondered what the whole picture was.

    Oblivious to your long half-mooned incision, we watched you lie on that side (ouch!) against the metal rail that protected you from slipping off the bed.

    As you drifted in and out, you reminded me of those young sweet orangutans at the zoo—quite blissful and yet scarily detached to the surrounding world.

    Dr. Helseth's brief visit touched me with a loving encouragement that gave me strength, despite no medical answers. When I wanted to cry out, "Where are you, Tommy?" I could feel you in the love of others . . . hugging me. It was then that I knew there was no time or distance in the Spirit. But the aloneness was real, too. It was like stuffy, stagnant air that hung without a sound, without movement.

Renewed in His Love

Dear Tommy,

The fact that you were *alive* kept us on cloud nine. I could sit beside you for hours—even though you were asleep.

One day that I felt such a pity for you, I realized maybe you weren't as groggy as you appeared to be. As you felt your head scar with your fingertips, I wasn't sure how aware you were to this sudden operation and all that had ensued. I said, "That's your scar, Tommy, from head surgery." You replied, "Duh."

Then, for once I delighted in one of those statements that most parents abhor. You said to me, "Pew, your breath stinks!"

Taken aback a tinge by your retorts, I knew you were alive and fighting. Your spunk and ability to rise up each time gave me hope and strength. Your faith was tangible. You were on the front lines. I could only be the medic. But then *again* the spiritual voice within you, within me, within each person who participated in your care or touched you did have a connection. The linking of the Holy Spirit with hearts and souls was grander at that time than I realized. The power of one echoes. And when we are under God's wing, so many people echo into such a swell that one does fly... one's strength is renewed as on eagles' wings. He renews us in His love!

At this same time, I had a dream in which you kept climbing high, high trees. After each ascent, a branch would sway you gently back to the ground. It was a comfort somehow of God's presence and peace, though my head really didn't understand it. My heart got the message, though.

Stopping by our former floor, 4 East, I requested some Bible verses from Linda—a nurse who had been an encouragement in that way. She wrote out Genesis 28:15, *"I am with you and will watch over you wherever you go,"* and she added Psalm 27, Phil. 1:6, Eph. 4:6–8. I had an intense hunger.

A Spiritual Guide

Dear Tommy,

Grandpa and Grandma had a chance to meet your behavioral pediatrician who helped you deal with pain. They witnessed him in action one evening as he stopped alongside your bed and spoke quietly into your right ear telling you:

> You have some wonderful energy in your body, Tommy—energy that will spread around and help you with your pain and give your body a chance to heal. Think about all that wonderful energy in your body, Tommy, and as you're doing that we'll go back into your room. There we see your lamp, your train, and the nice closet above your bed you use for a hide-away...now let's take a fun journey...

My guess is that Dr. Reaney was a safe person for you. He was a spiritual guide really—one who coaxed you to be freed of the victimization that you must have felt by pain, pokes, and surgeries. He empowered you to sail outside yourself—in ways your mind had power and control. That is how God must have dealt with you, too...through people like Dr. Reaney, but I bet in ways we'll never know until we are in a similar position in life where death pushes itself up close and wants us to move over.

Care Conference

Dear Tommy,

Nurse Tami had set up a care conference for input on your situation by all of your doctors, some nurses, social workers, and chaplain. At first the idea seemed great. It was long overdue. But my wish was to make the group small with Dr. Marker and Dr. Belani and the two home-care nurses, Liz and Lee, that we had worked with in the past. They were the launching pad to eventually get us home. Your situation was becoming less complicated in a way, because the organism had gotten more complicated, and your death sentence lay right around the corner. To get you home was the goal, and we needed no committee to decide.

Until brain surgery had shown good healing progress, your next eye surgery (a vitrectomy) would be on hold. Meanwhile, the pain control plan to use methadone every eight hours was in full swing.

Remember the day when we brought the soft blue blanket from the living room at home? It was one we'd sometimes use in the rocker. We thought the smell and familiar feel of this blanket would help. Perhaps its consolation was more for us. You didn't seem too attached to any *thing* ... simply love and tenderness.

So many surgeries! I had told Grandma, "It's one crisis after another! I don't understand God's plan really now. Pray for some kind of sign to show He is there."

One Little Box of Prayers

Dear Tommy,

Many times I felt ushered into the chapel by some deep emotion. I think I was extremely thirsty and I found a heavenly comfort in the serenity. I've always been so respectful of privacy and loathe snoopers, but for some reason that evening in the hospital chapel, my hands opened the little container of prayers on the altar.

As I unfolded each prayer request for different patients, I felt I was touching the tender part of others' hearts... of their own long suffering. So much moaning of love in one little wooden box. Then, as I unfolded the last paper, there was a precious pleading of healing and comfort for you, Tommy. It was from your twenty-one year old godmother, Michelle!

Candle in the Dark

Dear Tommy,

March 30th was your eye surgery day—the same Friday that your sister Maren was a participant in a speech meet. Her selection that she had memorized was titled *"Sick."* How ironic, eh?

The night before, Dad and I had cried a lot. I kept crying. By morning, cold packs did nothing to hide the swollen lids. Maybe we aren't as opaque as we'd like people to think we are.

That morning I arrived a bit late. As your nurse's eyes and mine met, Tami simply asked, "How are you, Jane?" Her words were an embrace, and at the same time a scissors that cut the thin veil I had mustered to hold in my tears.

There I sobbed. And sobbed.

Sunshine came in brightly through the window that morning onto your bed, but stormy darkness savagely swirled inside me. I blurted out, "I wish God would perform a miracle."

Then, Jerome, the social worker, caught my eye from across the room and he knew immediately my crisis was next on his agenda. The stoic Swede was crumbling!

Sitting down with me, he listened and we talked a while. I'll never forget one thing that he said. "I know at least a hundred people who would like to take away your pain."

In that moment, I realized your all-around pain had suffocated me. In acknowledgment of the pain I also felt, I was relieved and knew I didn't carry the burden alone.

After a little while, Jerome must have put in a call, because Bob, the chaplain, came by. I hugged Jerome before he left. Then Bob sat and I cried again. We talked a long time...the spiritual gamut of crying out to God with questions and hurting so bad.

One thing in the blur of it all, Bob told me to "Envision a

candle like it was God. He's always there in the darkness." In my despair, the thought sounded detached to me. But it didn't matter because in that moment it was Bob who was the candle in the dark.

A Doctor's Heart

Dear Tommy,

Your right eye haunted me. It looked like a dead whitish fish. Those eyes bugged me the most. Eyes are such a connection! To lose that sight—those vibrant gorgeous eyes—was beyond words.

As I waited over at Abbott Hospital during your surgery, Dr. Belani sought me out with tears in her eyes. We talked of our children. She said in regard to you, Tommy, that "This organism was so rare along with the course it has taken. We are off alone floating—no one to ask and compare with."

It must have been awful for these physicians to be denied answers and pushed to a mere spectator spot with such a disease.

The surgery went well—perhaps a cleaner one than the first eye surgery. The cheesy mass in the vitreous area was scooped out. Then after closure, amphotericin was injected into both eyes.

"I Have Overcome the World"

Dear Tommy,

About the time your eyes were in bandages again, you were moved to a private room in Life Support. I should say we were moved, because it was a blessing for us as well. By this time, having two doors to close leading into your room provided a momentary buffer from the hum of the world and others' troubles. It visibly symbolized our intense focus on the one life that we so loved and of which we were being ripped at to let go.

That room became a sanctuary and despite the disease and struggle, it gave me a feel of what God's refuge and shelter was.

You had told Grandma, "I just don't feel human today with all these tubes."

Dad likened your body to World War III and friend John remarked, "This is a medical decathlon."

A card from your friend, Matt's, family helped me verbalize some sense into this time. You told me, Tommy, that you hated not seeing. Acknowledging how horrible it must be, I said we were so sad you were hurting. I tried to reassure you over and over of our love and how special you were to us. On the front of the card were several Bible verses. One especially stood out. I told you that Jesus said, "In the world you will have trouble. But take heart! I have overcome the world" (John 16:33). I believe that you soaked that in, because I knew you loved Jesus as a child does . . . unblemished by a cynicism that age can bring on people.

Courtesy Communication

Dear Tommy,

Opening bits of mail for you became a drag unless it had some tactile object in it. A spring, money, or a fuzzy surface drew more of your interest. People had to be sensitive to your lack of sight and identify who they were as they entered your room, and tell why they were there and if they were doing some task. We all had to learn to be courteous enough to explain ahead in detail.

I knew somehow the "big picture" for your little life was brewing and its expanse I might not ever know. But I knew that going home was enticing to us all, so I began to dangle that idea to you in words—promises that I prayed I could keep.

The care conference date was changed—only two more days. I asked if you had any wishes, Tommy, to convey at that meeting. You said, "I would just like to be the one to tell. The one thing would be—not to have shots!"

Chocolate Chip Man

Dear Tommy,

Humor was once again such a key element in survival. It had been before in chronic illness these past seven and a half years. Now, it had to be sought for against an even blacker backdrop. But we found it...hopefully not at your expense, Tommy.

Maybe laughter and tears are closer than we think. Their expression guarantees some sort of relief and tells you that you're alive! I remember being in the lunch line and seeing the parents of another child who was on your unit. Yelling across several people, we dialogued and delighted in the fact that "Hey, my kid is off the respirator, too!"

Michael, from medical records, would rib me about taking all the chocolate chip cookies at lunch before he could get to them. We'd tease one another. I nick-named him "Chocolate Chip Man." He would, in time, write poems for us about our family and God's love.

Room #13

Dear Tommy,
As your nurse helped decorate your room with pictures and banners from school, church, and friends, I couldn't help but notice the room number we'd been given. Was it a cruel joke to have such luck? But I wasn't even superstitious, or was I? I felt too vulnerable to have Room #13, but I held my tongue.

Part of me said, "Maybe they gave us this room because Tommy is going to die anyway." But it gnawed at me. I felt jinxed. Then I remembered Him—our God who rises above all #13s, black cats, and broken mirrors. We are not of this world, really.

Suicidal Roommate

Dear Tommy,

    I recall one especially clear moment in LSU. You were dying. Across from your room, a young teen was admitted who'd just attempted suicide.

    A part of me felt an angry panic. I wanted to shout out at her, "If you want to give up your life so much, *I'll take it* for my son. He's fighting so damn hard to keep going!"

    Yet, I, who had had suicidal thoughts back in time, knew this youth's plight well. With a rush of tenderness, I so wanted to embrace her in my arms and just hold her.

    How ironic that as different as your situations were, Tommy, you and this young girl were both in great pain, struggling for life.

Messy

Dear Tommy,

At times it felt like things were *so* messy and sick. I thought about my lack of a green thumb with plants... and then about you. I couldn't even make my kids grow right, let alone plants—or so it seems with all parents and their children at certain times. The bad X-chromosome that I had passed on to you had created a disaster.

The organism ate you up—it had taken you away piece by piece.

> You lost your sight.
> You lost your ability to stand or walk.
> You lost your ability to eat.
> You were losing your speech.
> You could barely move.

And yet, sometimes I would imagine you meeting me one morning in LSU, healthy and sitting up and talking to me. A dream? I hadn't let it go. It was my survival... or buffer. Hope and denial continued to walk hand-in-hand. As I grieved for your body, I was also aware that your strength in the spiritual realm was incredible, that you were more solid, more in tune with life than ever before.

God's power in your little person was great. You understood well the passage in 2 Corinthians 4:16–18. *"So we do not lose heart. Though our outer nature is wasting away, our inner nature is being renewed every day."*

Rage

Dear Tommy,

"Come on, God," I'd coax. "Let me in on the whole picture." Hope, love, curiosity, faith, and anger battled daily.

Why, if He knew sin was bleak, did He even let man choose in the first place?? We hadn't done anything wrong (or so bad... had we)?

I felt I'd been blasted with a spray of shrapnel.

In my fury, I rattled on and on with a close friend over the phone one night. In relating my rage at the stained glass windows in the hospital chapel, Karen soothed me with her voice and told me how each piece of stained glass is so rough and jagged. When one puts those pieces together, the picture is beautiful. It's something we don't see or know beforehand. *But how did she know?*

We talked about how Satan attacks the mind, about following one's peace of heart. We talked about how the Lord has the heart of a father. It sounded good anyway.

She referred to two verses (Ps. 4:8, Prov, 3:24) for you, Tommy, in regard to sleep. And then, a verse that gave me the goosebumps ("The strong spirit of a man will sustain him in bodily pain and trouble.") Prov. 18:14. That was for you, Tommy! Bingo!

I just knew the Holy Spirit had conveyed encouragement in this verse to me. As your kindergarten teacher, Mrs. Henderson, has told me how sometimes the Bible is such a comfort and like home. You just want to touch its pages over and over. There are passages at certain times that certainly have that effect on a person!

The Panel of Glass

Dear Tommy,

A few days ago, I felt capable of smashing the oblong stained glass piece of artwork in the hospital chapel. In fact, I imagined doing just that. I was so mad at God. I wanted answers! How could God sit back and watch a child tortured and not intervene?!

Now as I sat there alone in the quiet, my eyes scanned the stained glass piece. In a much more subdued fashion, its worldliness seemed to taunt me. Then I saw it. A clear-shaped panel of glass was lost in the many colors of the whole piece. I hadn't noticed it before. My heart raced, and I began to walk slowly toward the altar, not daring to blink an eye, fixed upon this clear pane of glass as if it might go away.

The transparent piece of glass was different from the rest. In my heart, I found it to be a revelation of freedom. Like an exit, it blurted out "Jesus Christ *is* the 'answer.'" He was in the midst, often hidden it seemed, but together with us.

My body relaxed. I softened. In unison, I could hear your voice with His, "I love you."

Go Home

Dear Tommy,

Lab people began to be skittish and hesitant to draw your blood. People had grown attached to you, Tommy. Their reluctance to be any source of pain was evident.

That wear and tear that comes with repeatedly watching pain inflicted hurts badly. As I began to feel really lifted on eagle's wings, I bet God had taken over completely, and we were in neutral. There's a point when you hit that gear, out of survival. It's a time when you hope your compassion isn't compromised with some unfeeling mode. You were so hacked up. Eight surgeries to date.

I thought, "I must keep following the peace in my heart. The miracle is that we just keep on going."

And the suggested urging by Dr. Nagib to "Get him home" was right on. It wasn't the goal of living or dying anymore. It was to get you home—your big wish!

In My Arms

Dear Tommy,

April Fools' Day. Jokes that used to fly on that day lay latent... in respect to the proverb, "There's a time to refrain."

You would inch off your bed so gingerly and yet determined to get into my lap. You hurt enough to not even want to move, but I think you tried to fulfill our deep need to hold you. I'm sure your need was equally as strong, but as in childbirth, pain makes one disconnect to a degree. All your energies and spirit must have been so focused.

I was glad you'd been given a medical air-type mattress to prevent bedsores. You openly welcomed it. That must have been one more thing to make life a plus.

That afternoon I held you a long time—over three hours in the rocker. I almost didn't dare move in case I agitated you—or maybe worse, you'd decide to get back in bed. Routinely, my thighs would fall asleep, but it was a small price to pay to relish your touch. I couldn't imagine your absence and so couldn't compare that horrible missing you with that moment. What I savored would be in each moment. I sensed you were dying.

Forgive me for maybe talking too loudly at times—or too much—with too many people. I had to try so hard not to be lost in your silence. I wanted to fill you with life again—the way you used to be. But I loved you no matter what. I knew that all these years together were alive and spoken in the "loudest" form of communications as I held you in my arms and you huddled inside them.

I barely spoke those times when you were in my lap. I think you calmed me down with a peacefulness in that oneness. My sense of time severed connection with the clock. Maybe we had journeyed to a part of heaven and returned with some knowing that our Creator was in the midst. It was an eye-of-the-storm experience.

A fever halted the use of interferon.

The Bright Yellow Envelope

Dear Tommy,

Going home on pass at least didn't materialize on April 2nd. Maybe because it was Monday. But an emotionally explosive one it was.

The mail came. Among a couple of cards was a chubby bright yellow envelope. It was from John Graber, a dear friend whom I knew from a year's stay in the Cascade Mountains at Holden Village after high school.

On the envelope he had written, "Mailman, hand cancel this, or you'll break your machine!" Dad and I smiled. At the bottom it said... "Don't worry about getting this dirty. Solid prayers need lots of sweat in them. They are indestructible like your spirit and soul."

As I opened it, Dad, you, and I were alone. Excitedly, I plunged right in to read it to you guys. My hands began to shake, and my voice quivered as the following words freed us to weep...to hope...to feel such an incredible outpouring of another's heart. John dared hope with us and strongly so. It felt good to have him, whom I loved so deeply, take a stand.

> Dear Tommy,
>
> Sometimes it must be hard to pray. Sometimes it must hurt so much that it is hard to remember that God loves us and His Son suffered to death so that we would know God knew what our suffering was like and would take care of it by giving us new life before and after death.
>
> Tommy, I don't think you are going to die, and I made you something to make lots of the hurt go away. I call it "Christ's Hand," but it is really a solid prayer. I made it big enough for a man because you might want to use it when you are an old man. If you can't see for a while, you can read it with your fingers. It has four sides with one word on each side: HELP – TOM – THANKS – CHRIST. I used your grown-up name because when

you are old you might want to have it help you again. I was going to make it fancy and put a cross on the end with a hole in it, but I thought I better send it to help you right away.

Just hold it in your hand like you do the end of a ski pole and remember what is written on it. It will help you heal even as you sleep. Oh, I also thought that I didn't need to put a cross on it because your illness is a cross which will disappear as you get better. Though your sickness says "No" to you, God says "Yes." God is going to win.

Love,
John G.

Terminal

Dear Tommy,

About that same time, Dr. Kurachek, the intensivist on the unit had helped us see the reality of your illness. He said so many staff had asked him with concern, "What do you think about Tommy Wipf?" As head of the Life Support Unit, he had seen many come and go—a mix of sad endings and miracles. But he ultimately categorized you as *terminal*. The word "terminal" put some kind of deadlock inside my head. At the same time, I felt relief in that acknowledgment. In hearing and expressing that awful word, I felt power over it. At the same time, I knew then that no one would stop me; you would get home.

I knew the reality, and yet I had a lot of space for God.

If I let go of hope, I took away the energy to fight alongside you, who I knew hadn't given up.

The Odds

Dear Tommy,

There were no days off work in this game. So it was refreshing to have Dr. Marker return from a week's vacation ready to renew this case with you, Tommy, and so many other kids. I was *so* happy to see him! Dr. Marker hadn't let on to giving up hope yet either. I wanted to corner him and ask the prognosis, but I was afraid. I was afraid he'd confirm what I'd rather not hear. He didn't know anyway. No one knew. His philosophy was: kids can really surprise you and you never know what they'll do.

And we, too, had embarked some time ago on a pioneer front with new drugs and this rare organism. (We were told there were only two to three cases at the University of Minnesota—in the world. It would take eighteen times the amphotericin to kill the organism, and three times the dose, alone, would kill you. Great statistics, huh, kid?)

Sick Leave

Dear Tommy,
    Daddy finally inquired about taking two weeks of sick leave. It was granted. As Dr. Marker told Dad, encouraging him to take all the time he needed, "I wouldn't want you for my physician now!"

The Red Rose

Dear Tommy,

A single red rose lay on your table one morning, unsigned. We had fun teasing which one of us had a secret admirer—what a time to entertain jealousy! It turned out to be Carol in Admitting. What a neat surprise out of the blue!

We continued to take solace in the fact that we could call either unit that we'd been on anytime. Somehow knowing everyone was awake in LSU and tending you, helped sleep come easier. We dreaded knowing that at any time in the middle of the night, a call could come alerting us to a change for the worse—or death.

Seeing with the Heart

Dear Tommy,

April 3rd—Tuesday. Grandma was thrilled to have you and me in the back of her car that day. Wrapped in a sleeping bag, you were going home on pass . . . a luxury at this point that gave us at least the sensation of playing hooky—of making a choice so that we seemed in control!

You were dead weight as I carried you up into Dad's and my bed. It had become your bed, too, by this point—a place where you knew you belonged. Grandma helped tidy up. Then, Dad and I sank into bed alongside you and slept. Grandma left us alone 'til it was time for Grandpa to pick us up and bring us back to Children's Hospital. At that point, we'd rehook up on the IV pump to get the next antibiotic that couldn't be slowly pushed by hand with a syringe.

This time was a refuge for you, wasn't it? At home, you simply let go—you crashed. Your body relaxed, and your blood pressure improved. Best of all, your morale was gifted with quite a boost. You slept for about five hours. You were all mine—*my* patient solely. In the small basin that accompanied you home was everything I needed to assure your comfort—a urinal, vomit basin (emesis), nausea, pain medicine, etc. Plus, I had to remember to close your bile bag at different points. I was thankful that I'd done home-care with you in the past. I felt quite confident. I felt honored that the doctors trusted me to take you home. That affirmation from Dr. Marker in the past had given me a sense of self-respect that I so needed now and in being a good mom at home.

I'd check on your breathing often, sometimes worried that you wouldn't wake up. Dr. Marker had confronted me on the fact that in taking you home like this, anything could happen at any time. Yes, I was aware, but the risk was worth what it did for you, Tommy. No medicine, no words, no other place could fulfill these days, like the presence of home.

As you awoke that early evening, you sat up looking bewildered. You looked as if you were trying to cry. The emotion seemed dried up and stuck. I encouraged you to cry. As after brain surgery, only a few tears fell. I would never see you cry again. All that you had undergone must have shut off certain systems to survive. Or maybe surgery on the brain had hampered a portion of the emotional center. Whatever, I was in awe of how sharp and intact you were.

Then, you seemed calm suddenly as I sat with you on the bed and held your warm, swollen hand. You seemed alert and clear—void of any medications for hours.

The dialogue that followed is one I'll treasure always:

I said, "I love you, Tommy."

You replied so tenderly, "I love *you*, too."

Me: "How are you feeling these days about your eyes?"

You: "Okay. I don't like that I can't see."

Me: "Even if we don't see with our eyes, we can see with our heart."

You: "Uh huh . . . I see Jesus."

Me: "What do you see?"

You: "I see Jesus with a brown beard, with angels all around him."

Me: "We still don't know about your eyes. You *may* be able to see again."

You: "Christopher (a friend) is blind. Maybe someday he'll see."

Then I told you the details of head surgery—how close a call it really was.

You: "I didn't know that."

Me: "You made it and are alive! We were all *so* glad!"

You: "*I'm glad, too!*"

Me: "I'm so glad God gave you to me. I'd do anything for you, Tommy."

You: "I'm glad God gave you to me, too."

Then, you began to hurt again, and I gave you morphine.

Need I say anymore how these passes home somehow beautifully dissipated the horror of your journey?

Maren's Birthday

Dear Tommy,

Maren's birthday was the same day, April 3rd—the big #10! You were pretty tuckered out so we ended up having a surprise party for her in one of the conference rooms. Christy from "Child Life" helped make it happen and celebrated with family. Despite the gaiety and attempts to party, your absence was obvious.

Another Day

Dear Tommy,

Certain days seemed to be heavier than others. April 4th seemed to be filled with an extra dose of sadness.

The effort to get home on pass that day for a segment of hours almost didn't seem worth it, maybe because I was caught off guard seeing you so sick there in the kitchen as I washed your hair. Only four months before, your giggling laughter filled the room with joy as your chubby hands eagerly stirred the chocolate chip cookie dough. And now you weren't even eating.

A long nap at home was behind you and after washing your hair, I took my turn and headed to the shower. Ah, such an interlude! With Grandma there to be with you, the warm water from the shower seemed to take me away from the universe. The ten-minute diversion revived me.

You had told Grandma, "I hurt so bad"—a phrase that I was glad you could voice periodically, and one I dreaded to hear. You acknowledged head pain again as you felt nauseous, asking for the emesis basin. After your hair wash, I propped you up on the kitchen counter top and administered morphine, as well as an antibiotic. The latter precipitated, turning a cloudy white in the IV tubing. It frightened me, but I'd seen it happen before with a nurse and knew to draw it back out into the syringe. Then I flushed it with saline and heparin. I chose to wait and let the nurse give that med.

You were so warm and yet so patient as Grandma put cold wash cloths on your back. Somehow freshening you up with a semi-bath and hair scrub made us all feel better. I bet it was an ordeal for you to go through. Thanks for putting up with it all. Phenergan helped ease your nausea and sister Maren tried to help, adding, "I love you, Tommy."

How do people survive without the two phrases, "I forgive

you" and "I love you"?

Maren was excited to give you a flower that she had picked out especially for you. It was a Bird of Paradise. How timely; how like a child. You would become that someday soon . . . free to fly.

Maybe because we had so many unknowns stretched out before us in this earthly life, but I really felt at that time that death had more "knowns."

Its appeal was strong with Christ there at the end to lift you up and out away from death's grasp into a heavenly home. I was okay with that. Why didn't more people seem to relax into that option? Death is a horrific foe—that's why! And we have to wait to be with you again.

Back at the hospital, we rocked again for over three hours—tears coming easily for me, as well as all the way back home . . . each night alone without you.

"How much longer, God?" we'd often ask. "How much longer?"

Safe Time

Dear Tommy,

No matter how loving and kind nurses and staff were, the longing for privacy is inborn. And there were times I wanted to scream, "Everyone out of here! This is my boy. When he's gone, what will it matter to you? He's lived and breathed as one with me for almost eight years. Do you *really* care?!"

Rarely did I feel this way, but the feeling was real. Each moment was precious with you and I didn't want anyone to rob that time—like lions at a kill.

No one else was your mom or dad. There were only a couple of times when I wanted to remind people that they weren't your mom. I guess in needing to have help in taking care of you and you being so sick, both the nursing staff and I felt protective and responsible. Maybe it was that which caused a rare tinge of jealousy. But the interdependence with the nurses was sacred to me.

I'm a person who doesn't have a lot of boundaries, either, so for those who wanted to stop and see you—it wasn't hard for them to do so. I'm sure there were many who wanted to come, too, but felt like they would be imposing.

My heart went out to them all because I understood both sides. It was no slight thing that you had become a very special part of many lives. And it was a pleasure and honor for so many of them to have touched our lives.

And so, with respect to your need for sleep and minimal people traffic, our nurse made a sign:

> No visitors please!
> I'm spending time with my mom and dad.

Thanks,
Tommy

It insured some semblance of a "safe time" when no one (if they read the sign!) could enter. It mimicked a piece of home, a time to let down.

An Eye-Opener

Dear Tommy,

That night you were disoriented, perhaps as a result of an imbalance in electrolytes. When we'd go home on a pass, you were unhooked from fluids for about four to six hours, making a significant change. I thought, "Oh no, they won't let us go home anymore." It was scary to see you so out of it.

That night Grandpa had run into Dr. Belani and questioned her about Tommy. Discouraged, she said she had called Belgium about a new drug, but she wasn't able to get it. She had done a lot of extra homework for you, calling all over the country... knocking on doors that often had no further input.

That night, Grandma said Grandpa cried a lot on the way home thinking of you, me, and the whole situation.

One thing that was an eye-opener to me was that Daddy's parents (out of state) and my parents hurt for Dad and me in some ways more than you, because *we* were *their* kids, like you are to me and Dad.

X-rays and tests continued, peppered here and there in all this. Your CT scan looked real good. That was a relief!

Sarah's Visit

Dear Tommy,

Four hours' sleep the night before left me feeling woozy. And so a surprise visit from Sarah was timely. Even though she had come from out of town, it was I who felt like the weary, worn traveler.

What a breath of fresh air! All smiles, she seemed to light up the room in a wonderful sort of way. I could only watch. My reserve was gone. She graced us with garden flowers, daffodils, and an Easter basket of goodies from her folks. Then, she leaned over to you, Tommy, took your hand, speaking to you ever so gently about her son, Christian (one of your buddies), and about how brave you were and all. Her presence must have filled you with courage and energy. It did me.

After a time, Sarah and I headed to the empty cafeteria where she immersed me in a wonderful neck massage. Once again, I dropped my guard and soaked it all in. Like rubbing a painful spot on one's arm to momentarily confuse the body's nerve message center, I felt free from all my pain and free from cares. And in that next bit of time, we laughed and laughed. Old times brought up belly laughs that made me feel happy and refreshed... like the year we spent in the mountains, both nineteen years old and gaining a lot of weight! We reminisced how one winter night we ended up in the walk-in refrigerator devouring all the leftover puddings, jello, and desserts. When you live in 350 inches of snow where the sun shines only so long in the valley, this outlet was a sneaky filler for emotions—now it only too well provided a memory of hilarious relief.

Sarah's stay was short, but her love warmed us for a long time after. I knew, too, that she didn't walk away empty-handed. You had probably changed her life forever, Tommy.

Rock Bottom

Dear Tommy,

Coming back into the life support unit that day (April 5th), I ran into Bob, the chaplain. I will never forget that spontaneous exchange in the hallway.

My emotions were strong. I felt like a wild stallion. As I frantically rambled my fears to him in a nutshell, I realized suddenly how out of control I really was. It drove me crazy not to see ahead—whether you'd be meeting death soon, or whether that dream of you running to us in tiptop health would come to fruition.

Bob listened and listened. Then he asked me to lift you up into God's presence. He told me to image being still and letting God take all my dreams and fears.

Was I at rock bottom? It all made such sense. There was no other route but to turn my eyes fully on Him again.

Then that dream I had when you were in my tummy would come to mind. Jesus told me, "Be at peace; My hand is on him."

The hunger to be with God grew great. No greater question mark ever sat before Him in my life, but I knew I had to trust. He was there at the helm.

Bob answered my request for Scripture, handing me a list of Psalms and passages that I ate up. They were words I'd heard before—phrases that seemed to be limited by a certain era in history past.

But no longer. Each Psalm could have been my psalm. I understood every word of crying out...of refuge...of strength...of no foothold...of being in distress and a prisoner...of hope.

They were timeless now.

Psalm 77 (77:1 is the core of this Psalm) Call to God for help
Psalm 42   Hope in God

Psalm 143 Soul in distress
Psalm 142 The prisoner's prayer
Psalm 69   "Where there is no foothold"
Psalm 46   God is our refuge and strength
Isaiah 43:1–2   Hope in God—When you pass through the waters I will be with you
Isaiah 40:31   They who wait for the Lord

It dawned on me that despite all your sores, pain, and trauma, it maybe wasn't just You who was Job after all. It was us! Three years ago I remember *you*, Tommy, coming into bed one night and cuddling up quietly . . .

"Mom, when you were little, were you ever afraid of the dark?"

"Yes, I was, and still am at times."

You said: "I wish it was always morning."

My Bed

Dear Tommy,

You, my little guy, who was so afraid of the dark—now were blind... and yet, you could see better than any of us. Perhaps you had passed the point of even being afraid. I can only imagine God was talking to you day and night in ways only He and the angels know.

One of my favorite moments was after you had been sitting in my lap a long time. The nurse said, "Well, Tommy, shall we get up in your bed?"

Clinging to me, you said, "No, *this* is my bed!"

Being a Sick Guest

Dear Tommy,

Your medical records were getting voluminous. On one page I noted about you, "He is determined to do things himself." Yep, that's you! As I know many hospital moms have felt, one often wishes the nurses and staff could have known and seen their child well.

Hospital personnel usually encounter kids in a setting that often drains, frightens, etc. Like us adults, we hate to be seen sick and would just as soon hole up until it passes. In the hospital, one is really a guest, and for example, when you are nauseated, it must be awful not to be home and throw up in private.

Wake-Up Call

Dear Tommy,

An angiogram was scheduled for some days ahead, at which time your port-a-cath would be replaced with a Hickman catheter, so lab techs wouldn't have to prick you to draw blood. Now *that* was a heavenly thought, wasn't it? Keeping you informed had to be on the forefront of all our minds. It was easy at times to talk around you, but this was your life, your body, your dignity at stake. I think we did okay, do you?

Despite no eyesight, there were plans to help you cope with your loss of vision and possible long-term recovery of a part of it.

Your legs and feet needed attention as well to keep up circulation and mobility.

At first I thought the physical therapist and occupational therapist departments were an intrusion and in denial to what was going on in your room—in your life. I thought, "Is this a joke? How can you come in here and take over? What's the point? What is there left to do?" Too late.

But their suggestions proved to be wonderful. Not only did it build on our own awareness, but they also encouraged us with new ideas to enable your own self-care and comfort (massages, soak feet, change positions).

In that struggle for your eyesight, these people gave us a focus to hope in and act on amidst the cancerous black hole you seemed to be dancing in. It was a wake-up call.

Well-Wishes

Dear Tommy,

To think of another possible heart surgery in your condition felt downright mean. I pushed it out of my mind.

In an eager scramble to light up your world, people tuned in to your blindness. A huge cloth banner of pockets came from school. Collaborating with various classes, each pocket held its own special surprise (a tape of your first grade class that you listened to over and over again, magnets, a cloth rainbow with wishes, a little pillow with music to turn on, a squish ball, a puppet, coins, a plastic rubber Garfield, a shell, etc. . . .). I could tell you were deeply touched and re-linked with the world you perhaps felt had forgotten you. No way!

I was blown away by the love response!

The Sunday School at church gave you a bag of cards with cotton balls and objects to feel.

(No school today—Kristin and Maren were around—it was *so* good for them and you.)

Round-the-Clock Vigil

Dear Tommy,

    One night in this segment of time, Grandma and I compared notes on our crummy night's sleep. It was the night when I thought you were going to die. Grandma said she was awake between 2:30 and 4:30 A.M. Those are the hours that I slept! We decided that must have been an angelic vigil that night.

The Second Wind

Dear Tommy,

Having had a rough night during the white cell transfusions, you now (April 6th) lay in a deep sleep. Your peacefulness at these times was such a welcome. *At rest* . . . something you used to take for granted.

Like my dead car battery that morning, you were ever so still. How I longed to capture that Tommy smile or hear a laugh from you . . . *anything*!

The lack of response began to eat away at me. I sensed that your tears as well began dripping into a silence. We had finally learned that to be brave is to cry. But I didn't feel brave now. It was beyond any stoicism or in-control-ness I could muster.

You and I both were the ones in the family who feared darkness. It was as if we were in dread of nightfall, frozen in a stillness and silence that couldn't possibly be any worse than death itself. It was a darkness that I'd never known before. You couldn't just flick a light on.

Part of me wondered in panic—why won't death hurry and come? Yet in my longing for death to make haste and release you from your suffering, I knew I loved you too much in the flesh and couldn't let go. As I hung onto you, I felt like I was allowing your pain to remain very much alive. The pain was seemingly so powerful that I questioned what life was even left within and why did I hang on? As I clung to you, your body still gave me a safe familiarity. The sickness had created an emptiness, though. I knew your spirit was in a major warfare. I knew that your thoughts to hang on were much like mine, but your fight was in another realm of focus. I was with you, and yet I wasn't really. Submerged in our oneness with fear itself, I knew something was even greater than that fear. And that was the hope of morning time. God's love had been like that for you and me so often. Now as He held us in the dark, He asked that we just wait a little while longer.

His light was so brilliant in that moment that we were both blind in a way. We had to trust that He saw. He held us.

In that grief, a peace was born in me. And a strength that I had never known in such concentration reared up against the evil backdrop of the world that made no sense at all.

It was that evening, Tommy, when your second wind came. Upon waking, the nurse began to put eyedrops in your eyes. That action was the final straw in a drawn-out string of months of being cooped up. Panicking, you called out, "Mommy, Mommy!"

My tolerance level for the hospital scene hit the ceiling, too. I picked you up, disregarding our usual careful protocol with your tubes and sore body. It was an awkward hold, but oh, did it feel good to hug you—rigid, but upright and practically on my hip like old times as I stood and listened to you. "Go home, now! I don't like this."

I said, "You just hate it here, don't you, Tommy—all these tubes and all. You just want to go home."

Emphatically you echoed, "Yes! Let's go!"

Words had become difficult for you, and this broken ramble of phrases was a pure joy to my ears.

I simultaneously talked to God in my head as I spoke to you. I asked God to stand with me in bringing my promises to reality. To you, I promised I'd do anything to get you home. We would start up passes home again and then as soon as possible, stay home for good.

"Pray for his peace."

That was our fervent prayer request for you, Tommy, at this time. You looked horrible in many ways, but there was something different. Both Dad and I felt more hopeful—that maybe you could make it home—that maybe you could survive the odds above all.

Releasing you to God, our minds spun as we planned to look into home-care and get you out of the hospital.

It was like company coming over—there's an excitement and a rush to create order. And this is how it was for us. You needed a change of season, in a sense. You needed to taste spring. I could almost feel it in the air! I see why Christ categorizes Faith, Hope, and Love as so great. I knew the power of all three, but in this moment... *HOPE* outshined them all.

There's No Place Like Home

Dear Tommy,

Outside, winter had turned to spring with warmer weather. Inside the hospital, winter raged for you. Maybe in your urgent verbal declaration to go home *now*, you had signaled to us that you had stopped fighting. As I look back, you knew what lay ahead. You just wanted to be in our home bed. So, with that goal, we were determined to make spring happen in your life—in ours. It helped channel our hopes, because surrender is not so easy.

In one way, you may have stopped fighting the physical battle with the relentless organism—your number-one enemy, *but* it was you, Tommy, whose determination declared a greater power in asking to go home. *That* power you would not yield possession of. And the nurses were all in agreement, backing us all.

Being your primary physician, Dr. Marker ultimately carried the responsibility, so we had to make sure we could begin orienting ourselves around a sick child who needed twenty-four hour, round-the-clock nursing care and convince him that we could do it.

We met with sisters Kristin and Maren and two home-care nurses first, persuading Liz and Lee that the pros outweighed the cons—that by leaning on other family members and friends, we could do it (getting the girls to school, cleaning, laundry, meals, and your constant care).

The dialogue got us excited, though deep down I was on edge and unsure how long we could really maintain a child with your needs. But, I had promised you. The fatigue would be merited in the trade-off of having us all under one roof. There's no place like home!

Above the Clouds

Dear Tommy,

Leaving you at night was getting harder. Was it our last good-bye? Dad and I would wake up and meet you in our minds each morning. It seemed so unreal and horrible.

At that point, we were boldly asking for prayers of *complete* healing—whether that meant a physical one or one in heaven—we were desiring deeply your release from pain.

Rarely did I scribble down my thoughts, but on April 8, 1990, I wrote the following:

> Earth grows dim these days. I seem to watch people and even though I interact, I feel as if my head is "above the clouds" with God in a stillness and often in a peace. We were eager to get Itraconazole inside your body, Tommy. Dr. Marker mentioned that IV Itraconazole, the experimental drug from Belgium. He said he'll try to get it again. If not, he would fly you there. I said, "Yes, at their expense!"

We heard later of your interaction with one of your night nurses who was struggling with her relationship to God. One night on late shift, she asked if there was anything more she could do. You said, "Well, there is nothing else *you* can do, but you know who can—Jesus!"

He says, "Blessed are they who don't see and yet believe." I'd like to be the one who sees *and* believes!

Goddie

Dear Tommy,

One night as I came home, there in the dark across the street I saw a woman's figure approaching me. It was dear Goddie, our neighbor—the one who would give you candy and chat with you. As we hugged, the tears came. She told me that God will someday make it up to me. At that point, I wondered how could He possibly?! Her loving presence, even her words, brought a deep comfort.

Mommy's Psalm

Dear Tommy,

Perhaps it was the morning of April 8th or 9th. An energy brewed within as my mind, heart, body, and soul paced in distress.

At the breakfast table, I was moved to grab a pen and a sheet of notebook paper. Within several minutes, out flowed a psalm to God. I never erased a word. I believe it was from God—a gift to tide me over what awaited us in the weeks ahead.

Entitled "Mommy's Psalm," I would carry it around in my purse and reread it over and over again—drawing strength and being reminded of a vision bigger than myself. It would remind me of my dream once again before you were born, Tommy, that something would be wrong with you, but that His hand was on you and that we could be at peace.

> O Lord! How long must my
> child suffer?
> It seems a cruel path for him
> to endure for your glory, God.
> I, too, panic amidst his pain.
> My heart feels torn with shrapnel at times,
> cutting deep with cries that find no exit.
>
> What else can I do now but
> lay all this grief at your feet?
> Please help me lift my son up
> to Your Presence and let my heart
> be at peace.
> A peace that passes all understanding.
> Your understanding is unsearchable,
> Your ways beyond our earthly simple minds.

Yes, help me *hope* in you, Lord,
from the depths of my soul.
Pray the prayers I cannot pray
or know how or what to say.
Let me feel the special
refuge under your wings.
Keep me still there, Lord.
Help me know you are God
Amidst my son's pain and ours.

Help me trust and acknowledge
You, Lord, in all things.

Doctor's Embrace

Dear Tommy,

April 10—a morning that will never slip my memory. It was the silent turning point; the day that quietly slipped into despair . . . *the day that hope vanished.*

Experiencing "respiratory distress," I held you in the rocker as Dr. Marker questioned you about your headache and where you hurt. He ordered a CT scan immediately.

For a few minutes, I found myself alone, holding you close with tears in a free fall. Without hesitation, once again my words spilled out to you about heaven and that I thought God was going to take you as a seven-year-old. I felt free and as if I was being cleansed as I told you, "If you went there now, you could see again and run and play and not be sick. You wouldn't hurt anymore. We'd all be together again someday." Remember that, Tommy? I went on to assure you that "I could hold you, but not at night." I said that God can hold you all the time and that you would always be in my heart.

The time of solitude wasn't long enough. The doors opened and reality swept us out onto a gurney and you were wheeled to X-ray with Dad and me close alongside.

The challenge to get a CT scan wasn't on account of your lack of cooperation. I think you were so fed up, disoriented and hurting, that physically it just wasn't to be.

As your tape recorder played familiar music with the hum of the CT scan (that big doughnut-looking machine), we all took turns trying to assist in calming you down. You had done it countless times before with no problem.

Finally, Dr. Marker and I each held one of your hands. I forget what our dialogue was, but I remember alluding to us all coming to a closure and saying, "Yeah, if there *are* any more surgeries." I sensed this day would be the last one in the OR.

Obviously very disturbed at being a participant in this CT scan attempt, you slowly sat up.

It was then that I felt more for Dr. Marker than you, Tommy. As he held you close against himself—he in a suit coat and you barechested and in a diaper, Dr. Marker looked so lost and helpless. For a moment, his determination to get an accurate X-ray of your head, melted into an embrace—one that you held so very lovingly, so securely, and with such tenderness. It was a part of healing for both you and me that had phenomenal power. The objectivity and intense responsibility for you as Dr. Marker's patient dropped its mask and revealed what was always there, but not always so visible. The intimacy intertwined as a team, as a community was a spiritual source of comfort.

It was also this moment that reminded me of Olympic coaches whose high hope prospects for the games don't meet their expectations. The "stars" falter and yet sometimes you see those coaches enfolding them in a hug that all isn't lost. And your friendship with Jesus secured that fact—all *wasn't* lost. There was still a better win and an eternal gold of the soul and spirit.

Mid-morning during the scan, Dad and I called Grandma and Grandpa to tell them about our struggle. "Tommy looks sicker. We're trying to get a scan of his head, and it's not working." In between tears he told them. "I need to do some practical things. I must get in touch with somebody about some preparations as far as . . . mortuary."

As we bundled you up for surgery, it felt like there was a light bulb all around us . . . dimming and flickering with uncertainty.

As Dad and I sat with Grandpa and Grandma in a consultation room off the family room, Dr. Marker came in and said you needed a shunt put in. Dr. Nagib was all set to go ahead. Fluid was on the brain, creating a lot of pressure and giving you those headaches. And typically in your case, the goal of surgery was to treat pain. Dr. Marker helped us see that you were still fighting. We needed to fight alongside.

And so, a shunt was inserted under the scalp on the left side of your head. This tube would drain fluid from your brain. Then a small incision was made near the ear, and the tube was guided through the front of the body down into the stomach where another slit had been made. A soft nose tube for feeding was inserted as well.

    I didn't think anyone could live or survive all those surgeries. Man, Tommy, what a tough guy!

A Broken Promise

Dear Tommy,

Informing us that all went well, we also found out that day that eight vials of the new IV Itraconazole antibiotic would be available to you and were on the way from Belgium! Whee! Sounds like only eight vials were left in the world! Was this a forecast of your earthly healing—another miracle perhaps?! The roller-coaster went uphill quickly in that excitement. And yet, were we simply buying time to suffer more?

And hours later it hit bottom again for me as your new Hickman catheter refused to draw blood. We moved you around at all angles to see if the position would kick in blood. Sometimes it took a while for one to warm up, so to speak.

My fury inside screamed, "But there isn't time! I promised my son no more pokes. Have you any idea what that means?!"

Finally, a lab tech reluctantly tried a vein in your arm. It was one of my very worst memories. I'll never forget as the needle went in. Your cry was silent and it was all in slow motion. I began to cry because of the undercurrent of it all. I felt like a liar. I had betrayed you. I had let you down. I hoped your reserve of mercy wasn't empty. I wanted you to tell me it was okay. I was so, so very sorry.

Silence

Dear Tommy,

This was the fourth time you were on the respirator in two months. Your first words each time they pulled it out told a lot about you, your emotional mind-set, and the physical.

I remembered each time:

1. "Ice chips."
2. "Apple juice."
3. "Mommy."

As I anxiously awaited your words as the tube was pulled for the fourth time, I heard *nothing. Absolute silence.*

Some days earlier, I had realized that you were leaving us piece by piece. I'd scrambled to find a tape of your voice—longing to hear that precious (sweet, high-pitched at times) familiar sound.

Elated, I had found a Christmas tape that Grandpa had made a year earlier. Thank God for that recording and for one of the songs that repeated the promises of "When I get to heaven, I'm gonna walk with Jesus, talk with Jesus..." It was one I would play for you in the days ahead. I hope you weren't annoyed, but you're a heck of a singer... known as the loudest, too.

I so badly didn't want you to be a vegetable the rest of your life. You were comfortable with heaven, at least you sure had talked of it and God often. But when death stares you in the face, perhaps you were frightened of the unknowns and letting go of us. I told my mom and dad:

"Pray that the medicine comes soon.
"Pray that it works.
"Pray that Tommy's voice comes back and that
 he is in his right mind."

Two Visits

Dear Tommy,

So many bits and pieces flood my mind. I remember one morning when I sent the girls off to school with a hug and a "Good night!"

On the days I drove them to school, I'd often miss the turnoff to school. The hospital and you loomed in my mind. The focus was intense. I guess it was a survival that had no energy for much else.

Two visits stand out in my mind that week. The parents of one of your roommates several months ago peeked in. I motioned for Doug and Jo to come in. As I registered your appearance in contrast to the video-attentive, 'Fun-Fruit'-lovin' boy that they had known up on 4 East, I fell apart.

They hugged me and I did likewise. It was a time for tears. No words. Our talk of the heart was understood in the bond we had shared with our sons' health struggles.

Then later came Cindi. We had met only months earlier—my CGD blood sister! She was a chosen one as well—having the same genetic X-chromosome as I, passed on a disease that hits one in a million. We were instant friends—both free-spirited moms at home with chronically ill kids who loved the Lord and loved chocolate and licorice tea!

Cindi came to visit with the latter and a loaf of apricot bread. Her sparse words indicated she had taken in the situation as very serious. I felt her love—someone who had cheered me on in her phone calls, visits, and encouragement not to get dragged under by the "healing by faith" messages that came our way, etc.

Love and Sorrow Meet

Dear Tommy,

One afternoon, Grandpa Roland gave me a white envelope. Never having graduated from college, this brushed with the same feeling, as if I'd gotten a degree when Dad gave this to me. Of course it pushed some tender buttons that I'd sealed up often.

"Jane Dear, I was so often deeply, deeply touched watching you at the hospital (and Mike, too, of course) as you spent endless time with Tommy as his illness progressed. Just wanted you to know the background of this poem. Unending love to you and Mike, Dad."

Love and Sorrow Meet

Hour by hour and week by week
Month by month, God's will to seek
For strength to be a source of joy
To her hurting, withering little boy.

His plea for time was ever there
To run and play in springtime air:
Restore his sight once more to see
A friend, a bird, a flower, a tree.

To ride his bike and join the fun,
To snuggle in bed when day is done;
Awaken again in sun-filled room
To leave behind the pain and gloom.

But hour by hour she stroked his feet
And tried to cool the fevered cheek
To lift his spirit, to ease the pain,

To see a smile just once again.

If ever mother loved her child
If e'er compassion came alive,
It was in her, the faithful one
Who summoned hope for a dying son.

If ever woman vigil kept
While aching heart inside her wept,
If ever love did sorrow meet
In her, in Jane—
      It was complete!

Precious Time

Dear Tommy,

Dad's presence was *so* good! Working full-time up to this point gave him an escape from your world in a sense, and yet, I think as time went on, his doctor role became dispensable. Plus, I was getting mad to be the main parent caregiver in such a crisis over these months. Being your dad solely in the weeks ahead was the way it had to be. The only patient that he could concentrate on was you. Everyone else's problems seemed trite. Priorities and what is really important had smashed its face up against Dad's.

Time with you was precious. This time would never be again.

Unspoken Love

Dear Tommy,

We all tried to anticipate your needs and be sensitive to them. Uncomfortable in the silence of few words for so long, my paranoia ran wild...more out of fear, I suppose. I thought that maybe you were mad at me. Maybe I talked too much. Forgive me, please. Moms do easily become those targets of anger. But you were weak, and I knew that with me you didn't have to be "on." You could be yourself. That is a true friend. To be able to sit in silence...to just offer a presence.

I can't remember exactly when, but one morning before I got to the hospital, Dad had gone ahead, so I spoke with you on the phone. With such love you said, "I love you, Mom." That was the last time I heard those words. Though I longed to hear them over and over again, I had to trust in an unspoken love from then on.

After Dad and I talked a moment, he told me later that you frantically searched the bed for the phone to tell me to hurry and come. That image of you blind and so scrawny and all still didn't erase you. You were Tommy. I suppose it's like aging—thirty years later you still feel like you!

Grandma said when she called us at the hospital to relay a message, Dad asked her if she wanted to speak with "The greatest gift you have given me!" I guess that's me, huh? I'm lucky to have been given such a neat guy, aren't I? There is great affection between Dad and me. You were, and are, a big part of that, too, Tommy! Nurses would tell me "How nice it must be to have a husband who kisses you so much."

Being Maundy Thursday, Chaplain Bob offered and gave us communion at a time that fit for us. In your room we had a short worship. Bob included in his message the Easter eggs that Kristin and Maren had painted with the Child Life program upstairs. I took wine and bread for you, Tommy. I realized that

Christ's body and blood was the gift that you would partake of in the ultimate way shortly.

New life! How can one face death and not look beyond? Now *that* is sorrow!

Summoned to the hospital late that night, you had a CT scan due to more respiratory distress. Things looked okay, but meningitis was becoming evident. You had pain in your stomach, throat, and head. Dr. Marker and Dr. Sane were with us. It was 2:30 A.M. when we got home.

Earlier that day, Nancy, one of your nurses who has a southern accent, shared more about her family. I loved hearing about other people's lives—not the gossipy way, just because it is life and each person has their own battles to deal with. That's why that extra energy one channels into kindness and into the little things is what makes the world go 'round. And in time, I found out that love truly is stronger than death.

Amnesty

Dear Tommy,

 Your heart rate, etc., seemed good. But I knew you were constantly trying to cope with pain. Watching you in pain had a wear and tear on Dad and me, too. But the morning you declared, "I need morphine bad!," your pain was secondary for an instant.

 To verbalize that need meant it must have really hurt... but *you talked*! I was on a high as more medicine was administered. In those days, I got quite weepy. Dr. Marker understood that we were in a real quandary over this pain issue. He knew, too, that we didn't say much unless it was a real need. He okayed higher doses. He didn't badger me with questions. He simply knew and agreed.

 Once again, he told us the risks of going home. Anything could happen at any time. Yes, we were well aware. We all were more than willing to take the chance.

 I found it ironic that one of the groups we supported was Amnesty International—helping to be advocates to implement fair trials for people and to halt torture and inhuman behavior.

 In the "torture" you have undergone, the enemy wasn't even human. The highest medical technology couldn't even intervene. So unfair! And I guess unless one looks to the power in Christ, there is no pardon. He's given us an amnesty out of this world. It's there to accept and embrace day after day.

I Hurt So Bad
(by Grandma Doris)

  Those words of pain—
   I hear them still.
    They seem to persevere at will.
  I wish they'd stop

They interfere
And bring an unexpected tear.

Sometimes at night,
Oft in the day
    Where e'er I am—
    At work or play
      There seems no end
      Of time and place
    I catch a glimpse
    Of Tommy's face.
His blinded eyes that cannot see
Are searching for some help from me.
    I asked him, "Where?"
    I knew—his head.
"I hurt so bad!" is all he said.
"I hurt so bad!"
Words last I heard
From this young lad
    Seem softer now
    They don't intrude
    They give me little cause to brood.
Instead the words that give me joy
Are also from this same dear boy.
    "It's okay, Grams."
    "I love you, too!"

God's light is there.
It's coming through!

Bottles of Hope and Hospice

Dear Tommy,

The roller coaster of hope recycled its tracks. It was almost Easter. Paralleled in the promise of the resurrection was the anticipation of the arrival of Federal Express, which could come anytime with those bottles of hope—the IV Itraconazole from Belgium. (How ironic that friends of ours had been transferred there by 3M only a year before. Now their prayers overseas linked with ours as their country held the precious antibiotic.)

It was Saturday, April 14th. May 8th was the date set to go home on home-care—a hospice-type deal. It would include sixteen hours of nursing care from 4:00 P.M. to 8:00 A.M.

May 8th—that was over three weeks away. For a seven-year-old in your condition, it might as well have been three years. I knew May was too far away. I had a feeling you couldn't hang on 'til then.

Children

Dear Tommy,

You always were drawn to pictures of Jesus amongst children. I pictured in my mind teachers and doctors, etc. . . . who spend much of their waking hours with children. If children are so fresh from God, then those adults must be in God's presence in a very wonderful way!!

I guess, too, that's why God asks us to be as children. You just knew He was with us. You knew that His ways are His ways. You trusted Him completely even though your heart and head, etc., had been cut open.

Ah, to be a child! When Maren was younger, she once told us, "I know Christ is alive because I have faith. We can't even see Him."

It's true. Kids do know everything one needs to know to understand God. Matt 11:25–26: At that time Jesus said, *"I praise you, Father, Lord of Heaven and earth, because you have hidden these things from the wise and learned and revealed them to little children. Yes, Father, for this was your good pleasure."*

Now I understand why children cling to their blankets. They're a great comfort! Your blanket is in my arms most every night as I fall asleep. Fortunately, Dad doesn't get too slighted! He graciously hugs us both, allowing me that embrace of that earthly trace of you, Tommy.

The Little Things

Dear Tommy,

The little things! That has been the substance in my life, and I knew it was yours, too. It helped just to do the little things for you—like bringing water from *home* (in the jug you specified). And your appreciation was obvious. That water linked you with a place that you knew was real...a place that you loved...a place you called home.

I'd often tell you that you were like David, fighting Goliath. In death, the Goliath organism died and your fight was won because Jesus was waiting for you as you shed that body shell; that "spacesuit."

No longer did we take a day or an hour at a time. We took a *moment* at a time!

And one evening I especially remember an event that broke through the doom and waiting. Nurse Gayle, whom we had met some months before, came in and with unbridled delight took me by the arm, motioning me to come. I was in a daze as I followed her into the nurse's break room. There she placed her new baby in my arms. Ah, such a creation she was! It was a gladness that I knew well—one that explained the beam of joyance that radiated in Gayle's face.

* * *

It was such a comfort to know people were with us all in prayer, like even people at the blood bank (Brenda) whom I hadn't even met!

Stranger love. It, too, had incredible power.

Easter

Dear Tommy,

April 15. It was Easter Sunday. Grandma told me she was unprepared for Pastor Groehler's sermon that told about you seeing with your heart—that you could see Jesus with angels surrounding Him. Her tears flowed without warning. She said it was a meaningful and touching moment.

You had come home for several hours on pass that day. I told you what Grandma said. That even though we hadn't been to church in a long time, through Pastor Groehler's sermon, you, Tommy, had shared God with so many...hundreds of people!

For a moment you seemed to respond in a way that all your burdens had been lifted. I could tell you were pleased. You experienced joy in that witness, joy in your wilderness. It was like a big sigh...reaching upward to touch God...reconnecting with Him in His glory—waiting for you to be released from your tribulations here.

And so it was like Christ. It's neat how the cross can be made with two sticks, easily created anywhere...and a symbol of our vertical yearning for Him and desiring to be pure...and our horizontal—the flesh part of us that is so tempted and so human and so full of trials. At the intersection of those two sticks lay freedom, and you knew heaven would come some day.

You truly looked like Christ on the cross, Tommy...like you had been crucified.

Memories with you in time past lay in such a sharp contrast to the now. Grandpa and Grandma's remembrances of Grandpa playing the mouth organ and you pretending you were a rhino in the mornings at their house, singing "Turn Your Eyes Upon Jesus." Sara Henderson's memory of you at school, holding her hand, swinging your lunch box, and chattering away when you couldn't play outside...and you and pal Phillip in your white T-shirts.

Come On and Fight!

Dear Tommy,

I asked you that Easter Sunday if I could have some candy from your basket. I was surprised that you said no. But I understood as I thought about it. It was one thing you had control over. One sure thing you had a definite say about.

In time, chocoholic me—I did take some from the basket on your dresser. I felt such guilt. You had said no. But there was no way you could even eat one piece . . . maybe ever. It was then in a great rush of sadness and anger that I said to myself, "Yes, I will eat more! And then you will yell at me for getting into your Easter basket. And it *won't* matter because then it would mean that you were better. You would wake up from all this sleep and sickness, pain, silence, and blindness." I wanted that so badly. It was like I was telling God: "Come on—let's fight! Let's have it out! Leave the kid out of this!"

Taking a Stand

Dear Tommy,

BM's good—no blockages; new lesions; left hand warm and swollen and hurting.

Congested and very sleepy with a high fever again, April 16th brought our Belgium gold. Instead of the promised eight vials, *sixty* had been sent!

Was this all a big tease? Or would the brand new drug (not yet released on the market) work our miracle? Whatever, we needed a boost.

Maybe though, you were at a turning point and were quietly thinking, "Oh, brother!" as we scooted around in ecstasy . . . a gaiety perhaps that didn't even match with the situation.

While home on pass, we took care of your meds. One of those was eyedrops. As I made an attempt to put them in your eyes, you turned into a little pill. You obviously were upset. I hated to put them in, but as messed up as your eyes were, I didn't want to get lax on treatment, in case the future held new possibilities for sight. It was easy to think, "Ah, heck with the eyes" when your life was on such a jagged edge. I felt real bad, but I got angry with you and raised my voice—a rare occasion in your condition. As your anger peaked, you signaled your intentions to stay put at home. A rigid body told all. With arms tense at your side, pushing the back of your head far into the pillow with all your might, you wouldn't budge.

In the reality of this warfare, and in the relief that you had taken such a stand, Dad and I joined sides with you. As you lay in our bed, we took turns talking with Angela, our LSU nurse for the evening. One by one our voices cracked and we cried with her, sharing the saga of our little warrior turned rebel. With such love, Angela listened and fielded a plan to replenish our supplies at home, enabling you to sleep that night solely in our care.

Grandpa drove to Children's Hospital, returning with more oxygen tanks, medicine, and supplies.

You must have been aglow inside, Tommy—and not from only fever this time, but with a triumph; a "win" that only you could have engineered so masterfully.

That evening, Grandpa, Grandma, Dad, and I sat around the kitchen table deep in sadness, wondering the "why?" and questioning much. So much pain for one little fellow!

But I thought again of how after helping you verbalize such a low point that day, you had a say. It was about time, wasn't it?!

Dad and I dozed on and off that night . . . no doubt on a high *and* at the same time, wanting to administer our nursing care abilities with proof that we were capable and that this *would* work out long term at home.

Switching Gears

Dear Tommy,

As thrilled as I was about the new drug, I worried. It was hard to see the whole picture. It seemed cruel if you were healed temporarily by it and then had to go through all of this again... like just prolonging it.

Back at Children's Hospital, your head was in much pain and once again, meningitis was the culprit.

While you reveled in sister Maren's neck massage—the one who had the "golden touch," Dad and I met with our former home-care nurses and Dr. Marker and Dr. Belani.

Sitting at a large table in a conference room, I knew I didn't want to waste any time away from you, but it turned out to be a great meeting of hearts and minds.

Dr. Marker was one who always sounded upbeat and gave kids much credit for surprises—for healing unexpectedly contrary to the more predictability of adults. But it was the first time he disclosed that *you* probably weren't going to make it. It was like God had spoken! I knew then that it was a game of beat the clock. I wanted out.

The meeting was a neat exchange of launching us homeward. We felt love and support from all of them. Dr. Marker even gave Dad advice to take off *more* time—a month; a year even!

You wanted to go home. So providing comfort was the number-one task, and you needed one-on-one care, round-the-clock.

Dr. Marker had never had a case like this before. Making trips to see him downtown would be tough on us all. Hesitatingly and puzzled, he then lit up, drawing a conclusion that he would come to our house! He asked for a map of directions. Ah, the plan was a sure thing and now in full motion.

Giving big hugs to them all, it felt as if we were reunited in a new direction—no longer a frantic one in a last ditch effort to save your life, but to make you comfortable; to love you.

The Consent

Dear Tommy,

Agreeing to sign a DNR (Do Not Resuscitate—no ventilator or respirator) consent form was one thing. To actually *sign* it was totally different. Even though you were so infested with one of the most resistant aspergillus organisms in the world and even though no one had survived it, the consent was hard to sign. Somehow to give up in the fight even a wee bit, felt like we were saying we didn't care. I still don't remember signing it, but I did.

In Charge

Dear Tommy,

I think I began to act as in an emergency. One does what one has to do. I felt suddenly like Dad and I were in charge now. It felt good.

Asking Grandma to tell Uncles Dan and Tom, and Aunt Mary Lee and Michelle more about you was a first step in opening wider the reality of death. I said, "They should know that Tommy will probably die and that we are going home by Thursday."

I remember how happy you were that night when you refused to go back to the hospital despite a high temp. The decision was so right! Maren sat in my lap and sobbed, but as she learned you would be coming home for good, her tears diminished.

I remember thinking out loud to my mom, "Tommy is like a pure little lamb being sacrificed. I don't understand it!" Witnessing you, it was clear that this world is not our home.

The Good-bye

Dear Tommy,

April 18—Grandpa's birthday! To make preparations for your homecoming, the night before had been especially tense for me. It was your final hospital sleepover. I prayed and prayed that you wouldn't die that night, that at least you would make it home.

There wasn't much time for good-byes. So many medical staff were anxious for your well-being, Tommy, and all of us. They dreamed the dream with us and had united as a team to make it happen. Nurses from other floors, home-care, and LSU had volunteered to fill shift spots at our home to start us on our marathon... however long it would be.

One thing that helped was when several people all handed us their cards and phone numbers to tack on my desk lamp. They were still extending themselves as a community of love—making it known that if we needed them, they were available. By no means was it a cold cutoff, but it felt very, very lonely leaving for good.

I didn't realize the impact of that hospital community loss right away, but the grief of good-bye definitely hung there—and I know they dealt with that, too.

That day, I did record my thoughts. They simply were: "I'm either numb or at peace."

Under One Roof

Dear Tommy,

After four months, home wasn't even a sight for sore eyes. It was deeper than that because visually you *couldn't* see (you had sore eyes, but no sight). You just *knew*!

Do you remember what came in the mail that same day? Your supply of ants for your ant farm! Kind of odd timing, eh?

Within a short time, you were nestled in our bed. You had taken over our room and happily so! It was a funny feeling to see a bedroom that was a harbor of privacy and intimacy for Dad and me be filled with equipment and smells and people that in a way we barely knew.

After such a struggle to breathe the previous night, you looked so relaxed. Hard to believe that not too many months before, you had helped me put that antique bed together. Now *you* lay in it. I hoped the loud noise of the oxygen machine didn't bug you. At least you knew where you were. And that was confirmed when I asked the next day, "Isn't it *great* to be home, Tommy?" You nodded emphatically three times—the most response that I'd seen from you, aside from pain, in too long a time. I told you that you were home for good. I knew a "crisis" could put you back in the hospital, but I let the future just be. We were all feeling quite permanent where we were.

The feeling of contentment to all be together under one roof dissipated any horror of the previous months. We could even go to the bathroom at home and not miss the doctor's visit!

Glory

Dear Tommy,

    I remember zeroing in on your gorgeous eyelashes. After eye surgery, they'd be *so* short! I must have thought it a dumb question to ask, so I watched for my own answer. Sure enough, eyelashes do grow back it looked like. But I noticed one side was still short, and I thought people often don't die intact, do they—things aren't ever really in order... *really*. As out-of-kilter as you may have felt, you were more beautiful than ever. I would tell you how handsome you were, and it was true! I told you out of reassurance because you must have thought of that angle as well as so many other angles that we weren't sensitive to. Every once in a while as you slept, Kristin and I noticed a radiance about you—beyond the fever-flushed cheeks. There was a peace about you in those times. I believe the best word is "glory."

    At home now, we all were free to snuggle up alongside you in our double bed at any time. Good-night prayers, hugs, and kisses were special. It was hard sometimes to fully let go when a nurse was present, but we would ask her to step out for a bit or go home and then the place was ours as much as it could be. Sex sure may be natural, but death is not—at least in my experience. Its presence is vile and was never meant for us at the onset of creation. That was the miracle in all this that despite the horror, God's love still penetrated and gave life... *now and forever*.

    And perhaps that is from where my question came over and over again, "I have seen God work so much in this, but why does Tommy have to hurt?!"

    Though your voice was weak and raspy, just to hear four words that day was a rush. You hurt so bad and said, "My foot" and "My elbow." Perhaps the meningitis in your spinal fluid was shutting off parts of you. In the last days, you really had no bladder control or ability to talk. You were stiff and had tremors. Lumps were multiplying and abscesses like in your ankle grew more swollen. Oh, Tommy, it must have been so awful; you were so imprisoned! I have no idea how you felt. I hope I never do.

Overcome by Sadness

Dear Tommy,

I remember holding you in the rocker—times when Dad and I cherished with you. Uncle Dan walked into our bedroom. Not having seen you for a little while, he was overcome by the sight of you. He began to weep, "Gee, he's *so* sick!" Like I wanted to do for everyone, I wanted to protect Dan from his pain. Dad and he went downstairs to cry and talk.

I relished the quiet ... with you in my arms.

Suffering

Dear Tommy,

To care for you was a privilege. Most of the meds were pushed through between 4:00 P.M. and 8:00 A.M., leaving Dad and me a bit freer to do the basic stuff. I resorted to just being your mom. During that time, Dad's need as a physician was to minister to his son with the tools he'd been trained in... or at least to try. I watched Dad's inner turmoil—almost a panic to fix his only patient at this time, his only son. We both would learn that the physician and parent roles would move on to another type of healing and to let go of you—as you were on your way to the greatest physician... the greatest realm where you'd be healed soon and forever. Dr. Dad couldn't fix you... nor could we kiss away the hurt.

I thought about how Christ suffered.

How you suffered.

How we suffered.

In that shared vulnerable pain, there was such an unexplainable love.

Death is only a momentary separation with the backdrop of eternity.

As life no longer looks as good anymore, one has to even more wildly embrace faith, as the roots invisibly run deeper and further.

The Empty Chair

Dear Tommy,

One afternoon I remember sitting by you, Tommy—blankets and stuffed animals surrounding your left side. You appeared off in never-never land, though I think you weren't sleeping as much as we thought! We knew you were aware, though—your mind was intact. Kristin walked around to the bedside next to me, the tears welling up in her eyes. She said nothing, but her sorrow obviously burned in great pain. What was going through this eleven-year-old's mind? Hugs helped provide "answers" to a lot of things.

You were missed at suppertime. Though we rarely ate as a family anyway, due to a surgeon's long hours, I remember the first mealtime we all ate together after you had come home. Maren voiced her delight at being together as a family. Though your chair was empty, you weren't too far down the hall. We had our home back. It was a phenomenal feeling!

Dr. Marker's visits were brief but wonderful! He, Dad, and I talked a little about chronic illness and in contrast—the ordinary daily gripes we all have at some time. There was a unique richness in not having life run smoothly and "normal." He affirmed us and added again, "Normal is not necessarily better."

As I confronted him on *his* opinion as to how much time he thought you had left, he hedged a moment that it could be a long time because of the unpredictability of kids, but then he said three to four days. *Only* three to four days!

Not having experienced death in such a close, intimate nature, and run-down from chronic caretaking, we were in shock, I think, and couldn't begin to fathom death. But once again—truth had rung in our ears. *You were dying, Tommy.*

>   A time to be born.
>   A time to die.

The Round-up

Dear Tommy,

That Saturday morning at the Wipf household, Uncle Tom and Sue came, ready to serve us breakfast. Picnic-style with a blanket on our bedroom floor, we feasted on bagels and cream cheese. You lay quite motionless in bed, but I'll bet taking in what you could of the sounds and smells and touch about you. I know you were just happy that we were around.

People began to trickle into our home that afternoon as if God had beckoned them Himself. No doubt He had moved them to come. What impressed on my heart most was that they were children. Sahar and Sayeh, Kyle and Thomas, Blake and Leah. One by one they paused or sat... taking it all in. Some stood at a distance. Adam thought you looked like an "alien." Andy looked uncertain. He touched you as if he might get burned. Kyle held your hand. Two and-a-half-year-old Marisa said from her mom's arms, "I pray for you, Tommy."

Part of our neighborhood was in our bedroom! This is how it should be all the time. All members of one body. It felt so good to draw warmth and strength from their love... from a rubbing-elbows community. It made me miss the hospital's fellowship.

Tom and Sue got married!
Since then,
Tom died of cancer in '95 August.
Andy died of an asthma attack at age thirteen.
Sayeh was diagnosed with a benign, inoperable brain tumor.
Tentative is life!

Holiday Plus

Dear Tommy,

About dinnertime, Dad and I, Kristin and Maren had to "escape." So we headed to Holiday Plus for an hour. I so hoped you would never die while we were gone from the house. I know many don't get that wish granted, but I was so enmeshed with you, kiddo, and I couldn't comprehend it being any other way.

The store was huge. I'd been living in such a focused, narrow space that the aisles somehow were *too* big. In those hallways of food and merchandise, a vacantness seared through my body. *This* is how it will be! "No!" I screamed inside. I felt we couldn't get home fast enough.

The grief was overbearing. We sent the home-care person home in our panic for solitude, time, and more time.

Your chest was full of gurgling and rattling. I think if we would have felt every emotion we had, we would have died in our own pain. Too intense that night.

We paged Dr. Marker to unload our concerns about your worsening condition. Dad tearfully requested his presence. Though I took the phone next and told him we'd be okay, Dr. Marker came anyway. I didn't want to be a bother on a Saturday. As the wife of a physician, my mind often roamed to his family. I knew what went on in our own home . . . how stretched and demanded on doctors get. And both Dad and I struggle with saying "no" to people, so I guess I was protecting Dr. Marker.

So caring and soft-spoken, Dr. Marker just sat with us. Part of me wanted to be alone with you, Tommy, and yet it was good to have Dr. Marker, Grandpa and Grandma there for a while.

Please

Dear Tommy,

After Grandma and Grandpa went home, we put the girls to bed as we anticipated our husband-wife task of doing meds. Both well acquainted with the IV pump, we settled in for the night to take turns getting up. Dad threw a sleeping bag on the floor.

Grimacing as your diaper was changed, your legs hurt a great deal. We kept bumping the morphine up.

There was Dad again—another night in his underwear and a stethoscope hanging across his bare chest. What a sight! I smiled and wished you could share in the ironic humor as well. I'd threateningly teased Dad that I'd blackmail him with a photo! But your pain, Tommy, jarred me away from my silly image of Dad.

It was late and the room was fairly dusky. You couldn't tell me anymore, but I knew as you gripped my hand that you hurt so bad. Your eyes opened—those beautiful eyes now distorted and maimed by that ugly organism. I felt desperation and anger at God. As I bumped your IV site with more morphine, I lashed out to God in prayer. "God, please do something! Take away this pain. If you're going to make him well, please hurry, Lord; and if not, please take him soon so he doesn't have to suffer!"

Restless and anxious, I lay alongside you in our double bed, holding your hand for the rest of the night. You were still you, and in a child's body; but I felt as if you had matured and I was next to a seven-year-old who knew way too much.

Long-distance Dream

Dear Tommy,

As you and I lay in the stillness, my mind was alert as I listened to your loud, strange breathing. You were so very much alive!

Unbeknown to us at the time, my good buddy, Karen, in California, fell asleep that night awaking to a vivid dream. During that dark painful night, Tommy, as you slept, God was answering our prayer (it was just hard to trust and wait).

Two thousand miles away, Karen dreamed about you. She dreamed that Dad and I were holding you on the edge of our bed. You were limp but still alive. Jesus was kneeling, with His arms outstretched in love. Karen's hand was on my shoulder. As Karen awoke from the dream, she was dripping wet. She said it was all so real and poignant. She felt intensely that it was time to let go. Jesus was waiting for you. Karen knew that she was supposed to pray you out of our arms. She was to pray that we'd let go.

Even though I didn't know of the dream until some days later, we awoke that morning in a different spiritual way. Dad picked you up and your once rigid body was now limp as in the dream.

I told people as the day progressed that I couldn't explain it except that I felt some spiritual distancing from you, Tommy. *We were letting go.*

Surrender

Dear Tommy,

Grandma related her lack of sleep as well that Saturday night. How coincidental that Grandpa and Grandma were on "the program" that very Sunday morning for the Caring Youth Sunday! They dialogued from the pulpit about the Caring Youth Award they had just begun at church, honoring youth who had been neat models of caring. Grandma said it was bittersweet as Pastor Groehler stated that it was exciting to face the challenge of a new vision—and yet, their hearts were breaking, knowing of your condition.

That Sunday morning Dr. Marker came by. We eagerly shared our observations about you, Tommy, that we thought you looked a little better. He just listened. Then he listened to your lungs and took a scalp fluid sample from your shunt port.

Before he left, we shot the breeze in conversation. Then with tears in his eyes, he hugged me in a strong embrace saying, "I feel so bad." Then he hugged Dad, too, whose tears came freely. We three adults had given our all. That day we surrendered together.

God's Mystery

Dear Tommy,

Communion—truly our last supper—was given to us by Pastor Groehler who administered the bread and wine in our bedroom as I held you in the rocking chair with Dad and the girls close by. Here we were in the crux of brokenness... what better place for worship; what better time than this for recognizing our need for God!

God's mystery is where the "answers" are.

I smiled as I thought of my friend, Julie, whose son thought using nails for the crucifixion was "So stupid. Why didn't they use rubber bands?"

Christ didn't get an "out" for His suffering. He prayed, "Take this cup from me—but not my will, but yours."

Romans 5:5... "*and hope does not disappoint us because God's love has been poured into our hearts through the Holy Spirit which has been given to us.*"

God's mystery is in Ephesians 6:10—that verse in the Bible where it says, "*Last of all, I want to remind you that your strength must come from the Lord's mighty power within you.*" That you knew well.

Remember that wedding locket that you often played with around my neck? On the back, Dad had inscribed "Because I love you!" Fourteen years later, you spoke such similar words—a line that Dad says he wished *he* had thought of! You told me, "Mommy, you're perfect because I love you!"

In the Backyard

Dear Tommy,

April 22nd. For a second day in a row, we took you out in the backyard. We rejoiced as you handled a cough all by yourself—otherwise, we had to suction you fairly often.

Balmy and beautiful, the weather enabled all five of us to sit out on a blanket near the creek. You responded to the geese when they honked. Having you out in nature displayed the grandiose change in you. What a marked difference—to reflect on you scrambling up a tree or tossing a fishing line into the creek. Those days are over.

Christ Present

Dear Tommy,

April 23rd—Monday. I still feel as if I was detaching from you, Tommy. My need to hold you diminished. I kept imagining lifting you up to Christ.

I guess the girls went to school that day. I'm in a blur about that chunk of time.

My mind entertained a frantic struggle with the "faith equals healing" issue. I realized Someone bigger than a man was in charge. God filled the room, and I *knew*.

Dr. Marker's visit was followed by Grandpa and Grandma and four of their friends, whom we knew as well. I'll never forget the scene there at your bedside with Mary and Carroll Hinderlie—two people who had lit up our world for years and headed up Holden Village, the place in the Cascade Mountains where Dad and I met at thirteen and fifteen years of age over a game of pool! Christ was so real to me in their presence and obviously it was so in their lives.

Anyway, with Mary at your right and Carroll at your left, they each took a hand and prayed. Such love! Such peace! Mary told me later she sensed your time to go was ever so close.

In the living room, we shared much. Carroll brought comfort to us in regard to your pain, Tommy, as he told of their imprisonment in a Japanese concentration camp during World War II. He felt that Christ took his blows amidst torture. They had known a hell on earth.

Dad expressed his ambivalent feelings that came and went—wanting you to live; yet the continued pain. What would your quality of life be?

Walking in the Rain

Dear Tommy,

    As Dad and I walked in the rain that night, I felt a peace. I expressed to Dad that I wanted to be with you when you died and yet now it was *okay* if I wasn't. Then we talked about letting you go. The rain was soft and cleansing—a communion in itself. Earlier, Dr. Marker had said you probably had irreversible brain damage. We wondered if you'd had a stroke that previous Saturday night.

    Lori, our home-care nurse that evening until midnight, said she would sing to you. I took a photo of you that night with your teddy bear, "Rusty," named after our Golden Retriever, who had died only two years earlier of a ruptured stomach tumor. I'm glad we have that photo.

    We asked to be alone with you. In the back of our minds, we would always wonder each night if this was the last good-bye. Would you be alive the next morning? So, we said prayers and rocked. It was *so* good to hold you. The girls had hit the sack. Dad and I went downstairs to our couch-bed.

It Is Finished

Dear Tommy,

The next thing I remember, I awoke to the sound of thunder. Perking up my ears to the storm, I instantly thought of you and that you would want to be comforted. Almost simultaneously, I heard the oximeter machine go off (an indicator of possible trouble). It had gone off before, but my senses were on an all-out alert and sure enough, our night nurse, Kate, yelled to us.

Scooting upstairs, I followed Dad close behind. I paused a moment in the bathroom to yank out the foam curlers that I'd crowned my hair with. So, so rarely did I put those in and usually only when I needed a lift . . . when I felt a little down. A sign it was!

The moment I dreaded . . . and yet the one I longed for. How could that be? As I entered the room, I could feel you were going—as if you were waving to me in the distance. Dad had unsuccessfully attempted to suction you. Your lungs had filled with fluid. It was water.

Dear Dad. He, as so many other times, graciously gave up his chance to hold you. He'd tell me that he knew you'd want me to hold you. I'd feel a tinge of greed, but that bond was so strong. I accepted. With his stepping aside, I sat beside you. Right away I knew this was the end. Though one can't comprehend that separation of death beforehand, I only knew one thing. That I loved you. Scooping you into my arms, we settled into the wicker rocker.

Kate left the room to give us privacy and to wind up her role as nurse. Dad woke the girls.

I remember lightning and thunder. Your breaths came slow and labored, as if you had had it. And yet you looked *so* peaceful and actually seemed to breathe quite easily. Everything else around me shut out as I held you in silence. Part of me was aglow that I was with you. The other part felt a panic wanting to scream, "Don't go yet!" But this was it. You took a breath. It was 1:24 A.M. Then, there were no more.

"It is finished." A stillness. Your face looked tiny and beautifully white.

Then my tears came. I told you we'd see you again, that you'd always be in our hearts. Suddenly I heard voices again—Dad, Kristin, and Maren.

How glad I was to have the honor to hold you as Jesus lifted you out of my arms. There was a relief of joy. No more pain. Your long-suffering vigil had come to an end for you.

Dad said he thinks you waited for me that night to come hold you. I think so, too! But perhaps at that point, it was your way of holding me and telling me good-bye. That it was okay, as Christ's arms enveloped us all.

Good-Night

Dear Tommy,

How does one savor this time? Dr. Marker and Lee, our nurse friend from home-care, were called to come.

Like so many other times, my anger at the tubes was heightened by the fact that you didn't need them anymore. I wanted to rip them out. Dr. Marker was patient with me and was going to help close them off, but then I realized it didn't matter. I wanted to hug you alive without them! Dr. Marker couldn't fix you anymore, but in the candlelit atmosphere, we felt the healing of his presence and his compassion. Your blood began pooling in your back and legs as it drained from your face. You looked *so* good! It felt as if I'd said one thousand good-byes.

Leave it to Maren to change the mood. Within twenty minutes of your death, she had requested possession of your Ninja Turtles. We all laughed. She also wanted to be sure to write this all in her diary!

I was content. I was in shock and already switching gears. Lifting you from my arms, Dr. Marker placed you into other arms, too, that wanted to hold you. Then, Dad, Maren, Grandpa and Grandma, and Nurse Lee each individually held you.

When Dad finally laid you on our bed, I wanted everyone to leave and snuggle up with you. It was a tiny nick in the wilderness of grief—of the horror of your absence that hit later on.

After a time of prayers and when everyone had left, it was still dark, but hours had passed. As a family, we chose to be the ones to take your body down to Children's Hospital where that next day an autopsy would be performed. As we parked near the emergency room door, we turned the car off and sat in the stillness. Dad encouraged Kristin (who had not yet held you dead) to hold you.

Finally, consenting to hold you, she sobbed. What a load

she, too, carried inside. We were so thankful that she could release some tears. Her precious brother and companion had gone.

After a time, we brought your body into a room in the ER. Maren and Kristin, Dad and I—we all took turns holding you again. Where were you at that time, Tommy? Could you see us? I suppose we took forever, huh?

Dad and the girls began to walk out into the hall. Anyway, I kissed you a bunch of times on those soft cheeks of yours. And as daylight broke, we decided to move on. Trying to gently lay you on the table, there you were in only your light blue cartoon pajama bottoms. It didn't seem right to leave you. There was no transition—it felt abrupt. I'd rather have laid you on a bed at least. I kissed you again and again on both cheeks and in a daze, I made myself go. How does one decide which kiss will be the last? How do you decide at what moment to let go? We just left you all alone. How do you decide not to look back? And if you do look back, how could you ever leave?

Robot-like, I didn't look back. But as I paused in the doorway, the heavenly Father Himself must have spiritually reassured me that He had taken over now because no parent in their right mind would leave their child.

Remembering a night when I'd put you to bed and had curled up in a hug alongside you with your back to me in blissful silence, I was sure you were asleep. You suddenly turned to me and said so sweetly, "Mom, I won't ever forget you!"

Now it was my turn. I won't forget you either! We will see each other again. Now for you it is always morning. Goodnight, Tommy.

It was the middle of the night. Many months earlier, my son had been buried in his favorite blue jeans. The unbearable pain of his absence often kept me awake. How could I possibly continue life without him? As my heart leaked out its silent cry, a figure silhouetted in light sat next to me on my bed. Fear, awe, and reverence filled me. He said, *"Draw near to me and I will draw near to you."* Then, he was gone.

Rejoice not over me, O my enemy;
When I fall, I shall rise;
When I sit in darkness,
The Lord will be a light to me.
      —Micah 7:8

Grief

Like a chunk of glass, severed from its main source,
I am attacked at all angles.
    In the dark with sweeping cuts
        The blade strikes me over and over again.
No time to think as I shut my eyes wanting it to be finished
. . . Taut and terrified, I shudder
      As I grow smaller
      Full of changes
      No longer familiar to myself.
I lie on a table waiting.
Time is silent.
Suddenly, I am picked up by the One who has shaved me into diamond-shaped sides.
    His hands are soft.
Though I hadn't felt it before,
I now sense they were always gentle and loving.
      He calls me a prism.
        A silver cord laced through a tiny hole completes my
            being as He places me high on the window—a spot
            He has chosen.
In time, His Light rises with the morning.
      I wait.
Then His Light beams throughout my newly shaped body of glass.
I feel passion and warmth
As the light churns colors within me exploding them all across the room . . .
Dancing on the blade that has carved new life into my body and soul.

    (A poem I wrote some years after Tommy died.)